At Savannah/Hilton Head International, you can choose from seven airlines offering nonstop service to a variety of major cities.

AIR CANADA · allegiant · American Airlines · DELTA
jetBlue · sun country airlines · UNITED

flySAV.com

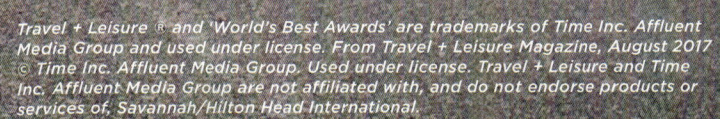

Travel + Leisure ® and 'World's Best Awards' are trademarks of Time Inc. Affluent Media Group and used under license. From Travel + Leisure Magazine, August 2017 © Time Inc. Affluent Media Group. Used under license. Travel + Leisure and Time Inc. Affluent Media Group are not affiliated with, and do not endorse products or services of, Savannah/Hilton Head International.

table of contents

5
SAVANNAH'S ART & SOUL

10
SAVANNAH'S PICTURESQUE PLACES

12
SHOPPING IN SAVANNAH

14
DON'T FORGET

19
5 THINGS YOU CAN DO RIGHT NOW IN SAVANNAH

29
7 THINGS SAVANNAH HAD FIRST

30
EXPERIENCE THE GREAT OUTDOORS IN SAVANNAH

33
VISIT TYBEE ISLAND

40
WELCOME TO THE GOLDEN ISLES

44
SAVANNAH'S SCARY SIDE

46
GETTING AROUND SAVANNAH

51
CITY MARKET

57
FINDING ROMANCE IN SAVANNAH

60
TOP TEN REASONS YOU NEED
TO MAKE YOUR WAY DOWN TO RIVER STREET

65
COASTAL CUISINE FOR THE FOODIE IN YOU

76
WHAT DO YOU WANT TO DRINK?

78
GOURMET FUN: THE SAVANNAH FOOD & WINE FESTIVAL

82
TASTES OF SAVANNAH

84
STEP INSIDE THESE 3 SACRED SAVANNAH SPOTS

89
READY TO CALL SAVANNAH HOME?

from the publisher

"I enjoy the walkability and beauty of Savannah as well as photographing its many picturesque views."

- Rebecca Fenwick

Welcome to our beautiful, historic Savannah founded in 1733. We're so delighted you're here.

Maybe you came to Savannah for time with family or friends, or maybe you're here for business, or maybe you, like the photographer of our cover photo, came to Savannah for the history. Whatever the reason, you're in the right place to find just what you're looking for. And, we're here to help you on your southern journey.

The easiest way to get started might be a midday stroll through Savannah. That's where Rebecca Fenwick found the cover photo of Orleans Square. "I am a lover of history, architecture, and the outdoors and am a historic preservation specialist. I enjoy the walkability and beauty of Savannah as well as photographing its many picturesque views," said Fenwick.

Orleans Square is known for its gorgeous green fountain, installed in 1989—the same year as the 250th anniversary of Savannah's founding. The fountain commemorates the contributions of early German immigrants to colonial Georgia. The square, itself, was named in 1815 to recognize the victory at the Battle of New Orleans in the War of 1812.

Around the fountain, I encourage you to go have a seat on one of the benches and just take in your historic surroundings. When you're ready to go explore, come back here and we'll help you find your next adventure, place to dine and shop. We're so glad you've come to Savannah!

Michael Owens, Publisher

On the cover: "Orleans Square" photographed by Rebecca Fenwick

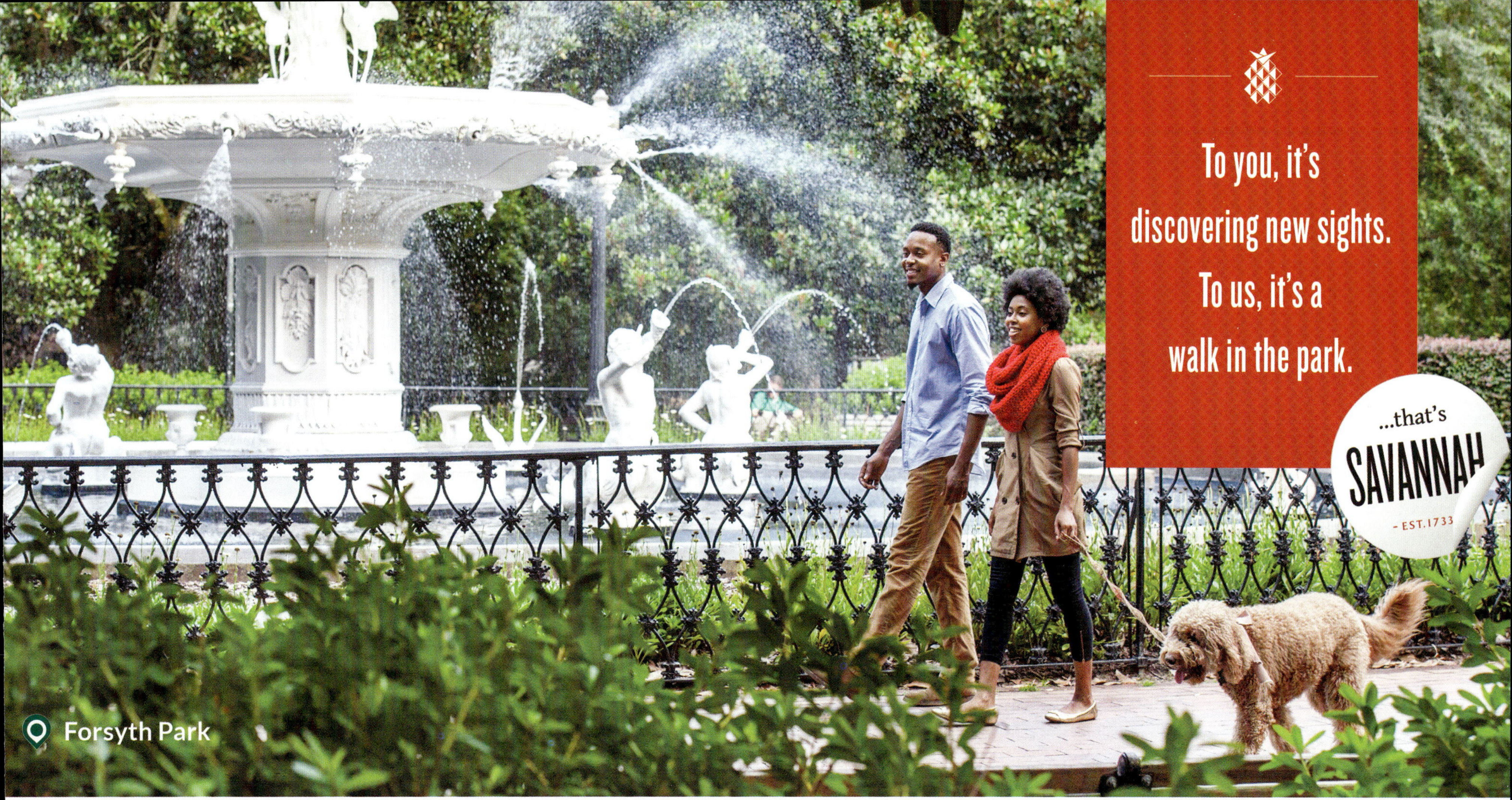

To you, it's discovering new sights. To us, it's a walk in the park.

...that's SAVANNAH - EST. 1733

Forsyth Park

TRAVEL TIPS

Be inspired and discover special offers at **VisitSavannah.com**.

Begin your visit at our **Main Visitor Center** at 301 Martin Luther King Blvd.

Join the conversation by posting your photos and tagging **#VisitSavannah**.

SAVANNAH'S *Art & Soul*

Savannah serves as a true haven for creativity. Nestled along the South Atlantic coast, Georgia's First City warmly embraces the arts, nurturing emerging talent and celebrating a world of beauty.

When a city itself is a work of art, it's not surprising to find it full of artistic and cultural offerings. As you begin your southern journey through our historic town, take notice of the rich history of art that beckons back to our founding in 1733.

Since that time, Savannah has attracted artists and aesthetes far and wide. In fact, historians say Savannah has the richest legacy among cities in the state of providing access to and supporting art. And, it's only grown steadily over the last four decades, anchored by the Savannah College of Art and Design's success and fueled by a growing appetite for original work by talented local artists.

From folk art to fine music, visitors can enjoy something for every taste in Georgia's First City. Here are a few must-see stops along your southern journey.

{ THE ART CENTER AT CITY MARKET }

Traditional and contemporary influences meet sparkle and whimsy among the dozens of galleries and studios that make up this community of artists and craftsmen. Observe painters, sculptors and textile artists at work in dozens of studios. There are even more galleries along City Market's open-air walkways—an entire day can be spent exploring this historic site known as "The Art and Soul of Savannah." Free and open to the public.

Jefferson Street at West St. Julian Street | 912.232.4903
SAVANNAHCITYMARKET.COM

{ ROOTS UP GALLERY }

Roots Up Gallery specializes in showcasing the works of folk art and will provide you with a one-of-a-kind souvenir. You'll also discover a wonderful array of paintings, sculptures, pottery and jewelry from local and regional artists. This art form can be complex or simple in nature, and is as expressive as the Blues, a genre that recounts memories, hardships, love and loss.

412-C Whitaker Street | 912.677.2845
ROOTSUPGALLERY.COM

{ SAVANNAH PHILHARMONIC }

For musical arts, check out a Savannah Philharmonic performance. This professional orchestra presents a full range of concerts each season (September to May), from classics to pops. You may hear a wide range of concerts, including fully-staged operas, several oratorios, pops concerts, chamber concerts, classical symphonies and concerti by beloved composers including Beethoven, Stravinsky, Gershwin, Abba, Elton John, McCartney, Brahms, Tchaikovsky, Schostakovich, Rachmaninoff, and many others.

1515 Abercorn Street | 912.232.6002
SAVANNAHPHILHARMONIC.ORG

{ THE TELFAIR MUSEUM IS THE OLDEST PUBLIC ART MUSEUM IN THE SOUTH }

{ TIFFANI TAYLOR GALLERY }

Set in the heart of the historic district, Tiffani Taylor's Gallery creates an inviting and vibrant atmosphere to showcase her equally as welcoming artwork. Her signature red poppies dance along the walls while flecks of gold leaf catch rays of sunlight that stray in through the tall arched windows. So, whether you're an experienced collector, or just enjoy gallery hopping, stop by the Tiffani Taylor Gallery and see what's captured the eyes of so many.

11 Whitaker Street | 912.507.7860
TIFFANIART.COM

{ SCAD MUSEUM OF ART }

A world-renowned art and design school makes finding art in this city easy. Check out the rotating exhibits at the premier contemporary art museum, SCAD Museum of Art. You'll see works from students and masters alike. The exhibits rotate on the school's quarter system.

601 Turner Boulevard | 912.525.7191
SCADMOA.ORG

{ TELFAIR ACADEMY }

The Telfair Museum is the oldest public art museum in the South. The legacy of one visionary Savannahian, it was founded in 1883 through the bequest of prominent local philanthropist Mary Telfair, who left her home and its furnishings to the Georgia Historical Society to be opened as a museum. Today, Telfair Museums consists of three unique buildings: the Telfair Academy and the Owens-Thomas House, two National Historic Landmark sites built in the early nineteenth century, and the contemporary Jepson Center. *(left)*

121 Barnard Street
TELFAIR.ORG

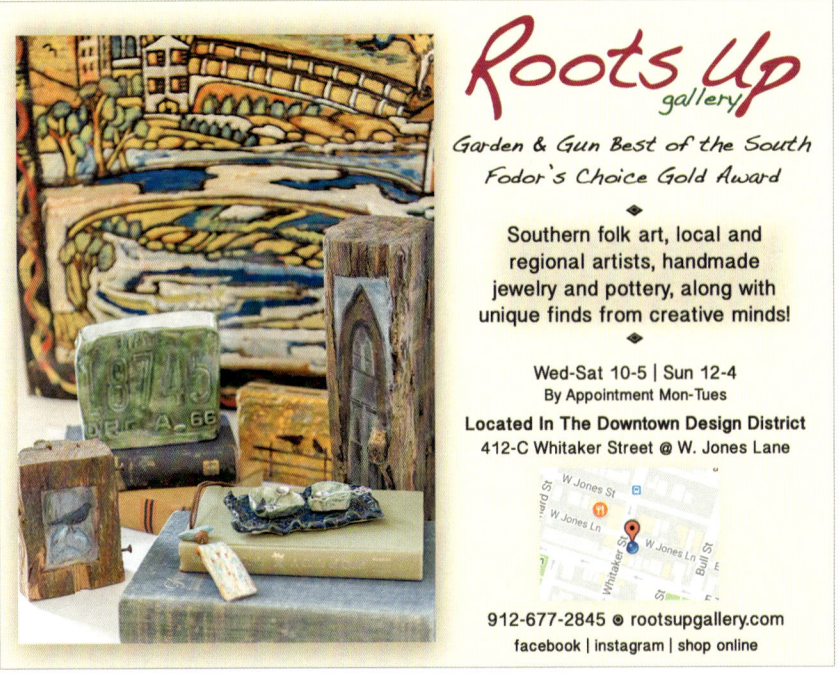

These days, photos aren't contained to mere photo albums, but shared instantly with the world via any number of social media outlets. The good news is, Savannah abounds with picturesque locales – but it can be hard to narrow them down. Our best advice is to set out on a tour, keep your eyes peeled for these prime points of interests and we guarantee you'll return home with beautiful memories of your Savannah stay.

{ FORSYTH FOUNTAIN }

Serving as the backdrop to many a gorgeous wedding, the Forsyth Fountain in Forsyth Park ensures you will capture a stunning photo every time. *(right)*

{ SQUARES }

With 22 squares to choose from, all relatively close together, you will have any number of fountains, gazebos, statues and oak-tree canopies to make even amateur photographers feel like a pro. *(Chippewa Square, left)*

{ TYBEE ISLAND }

Sunrise, sunset and every hour in between, the beaches of Tybee will have you in rapid-shutter mode. *(below)*

{ CATHEDRAL OF ST. JOHN THE BAPTIST }

With its towering dual steeples, ornate architecture and stunning stained-glass windows, this historic place of worship is a must on every photographer's list.

{ BONAVENTURE CEMETERY }

We know, it may seem a bit creepy, but the ornate headstones and sculptures of this historic resting place may just have you seeing cemeteries in a whole new light.

{ ISLE OF HOPE }

Just a short drive from Downtown Savannah you'll discover Isle of Hope. With its Martha's Vineyard appeal and Lowcountry charm, this tucked away community is known for its inspired vistas of coastal marshlands at every turn. Be sure to also make a stop at nearby Wormsloe Historic Site offering a breathtaking entry of live oaks and Spanish moss that lead to the tabby ruins of this historic plantation.

Shopping
IN SAVANNAH

ONE OF THE THINGS WE LOVE TO DO IN SAVANNAH? SHOP.

From one-of-a-kind art pieces to handmade soaps, stores you love, stores you don't yet know and even rare antiques, there is certainly no shortage of options to find that perfect something. Here's a guide to some of our shopping districts.

{ BROUGHTON STREET }

This historic street has always been the hub of shopping for Savannah, and it shows no signs of slowing. Intermingled with brand names are local retailers you're sure to love. During the holidays, this street lights up the night sky in a big way. *(above)*

{ SAVANNAH RIVERFRONT }

Find everything including Savannah books, Civil War artifacts, Southern gourmet selections, art, antiques and more.

{ CITY MARKET }

Browse City Market's eclectic blend of art galleries and specialty shops that fill every nook and cranny of this part of the Historic District.

{ GREATER SAVANNAH }

Outside of the Historic District, Savannah boasts two malls along with several outdoor shopping centers where you will find all the brand names you love — and more!

Like the city itself, Savannah's shops are a fusion of countless styles and influences, from Lowcountry quaint to cosmopolitan chic to art school underground. Hit the cobblestones and you'll discover a million ways to take home a slice of Savannah.

spartina 449
Daufuskie Island, SC

spartina449.com

Our luxurious colorful linen and leather accessories are inspired by the rich history and natural beauty of the South Carolina & Georgia Lowcountry.

Spartina's Savannah Store
317 W. BROUGHTON ST.
Downtown Savannah

Don't Forget

5 Things to Help You Remember Your Trip

© Hilton Head Chamber of Commerce

Wish you could extend your stay in Savannah? We do too. We love having you here, but if you have to go home. Be sure to take a piece of Savannah with you. Remember your trip to Savannah with one of these fabulous finds.

{ GULLAH STRAW BASKET }

Culture, function and beauty combine in these handcrafted creations that are a signature of the Lowcountry. The art originated in Sierra Leone, West Africa but was handed down to descendants of enslaved African people, known as Gullah; a tradition that continues to this day. *(left)*

{ ANTIQUES }

With a city this old, we have hundreds of years' worth of antiques for you to treasure. Whether you find a beautiful tapestry or your new favorite table, there are so many reasons to check out our antique stores. And, many of them will ship to your home, so you're not stuck trying to fit it in your carryon luggage. One of our favorites is Victory Antiques in midtown.

{ JEWELRY }

With every gem wrapped in a signature navy box, you know Levy Jewelers will make your remembrance of Savannah unforgettable. After all, this family has been providing the community with jewelry for 117 years. It's a true Savannah staple with its flagship building in the Broughton street shopping district.

{ GEORGIA WINE }

Before America was a sovereign nation, the British had eyes on Georgia as the wine capital of the new colonies. Nearly 300 years later, we're celebrating our rich wine history with some spectacular local wines. Share our hidden secret with your loved ones.

{ SAVANNAH BOOK }

What's the best way to share your Savannah experience? With a book that starts the conversations with friends about your wonderful trip. Local book retailers are peppered throughout the city where you can pick up your favorite version of this book, Savannah: A Southern Journey. Or, just order your own copy at TourismLeadershipCouncil.com.

{ JOHNNY MERCER WROTE "MOON RIVER" AND NEARLY 1,400 OTHER SONGS }

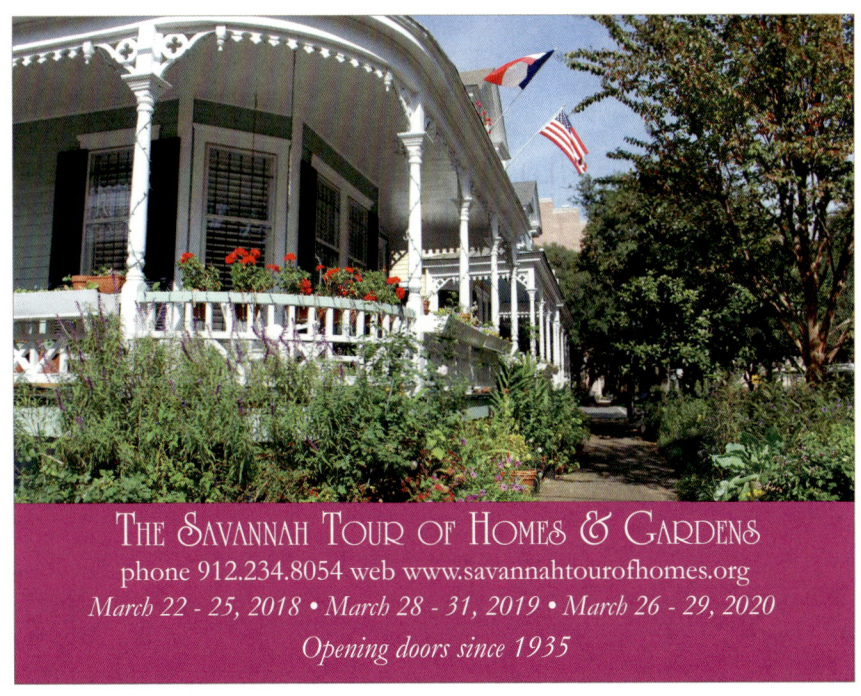
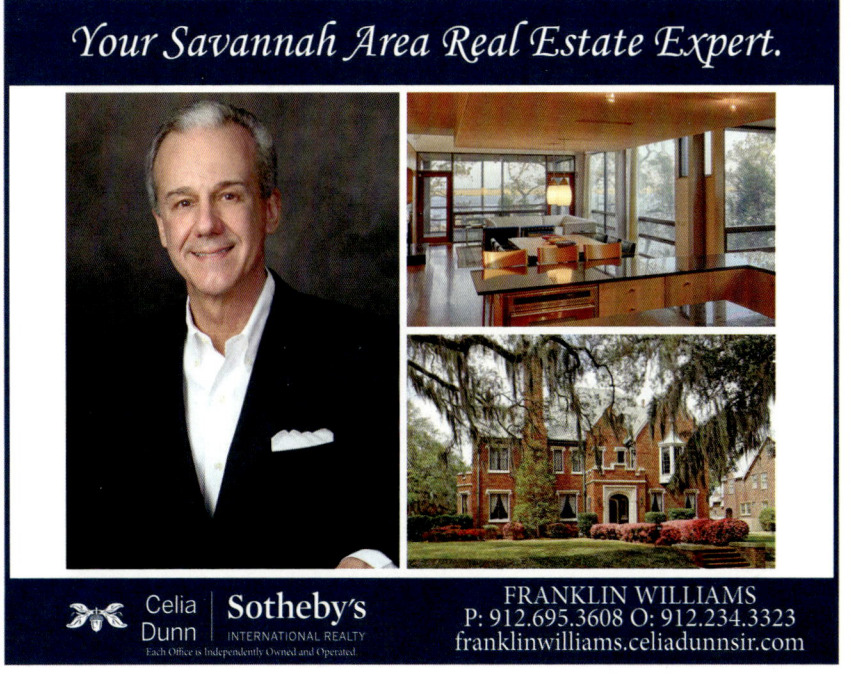

 SAVANNAH HISTORY MUSEUM — explore history

 SAVANNAH CHILDREN'S MUSEUM — play & learn

 OLD FORT JACKSON — experience life as a soldier

 PINPOINT HERITAGE MUSEUM — discover life on the water

 GEORGIA STATE RAILROAD MUSEUM — ride the rails

 CHS A Coastal Heritage Society Experience

www.chsgeorgia.org

FIVE THINGS
YOU CAN DO IN SAVANNAH
Right Now

In Savannah, history and adventure await around every corner. But, if you need a little inspiration to find something to do, then try five of our top picks for interactive fun.

savannah: a southern journey | 19

{ LEARN TO COOK LIKE THE PROS }

Don't just go out to eat, make your food in a fun, interactive, hands-on cooking class where you'll make a complete meal—dessert and all. If you've been cooking for years or simply want to gain confidence in the kitchen, in these classes you'll discuss food, cook together, laugh, share stories, learn techniques, understand ingredients and be inspired to make some amazing Southern dishes back home.

CHEF DARIN'S KITCHEN TABLE HANDS-ON COOKING CLASSES
2514 Abercorn Street #140 | 912.662.6882 | chefdarin.com

{ BOARD A BOAT }

Living in coastal Georgia, means you grow up on the water, so do what the locals do and get in a boat. You can head out on a sunset cruise, inshore or deep-sea fishing, or watch the bottlenose dolphins playing in their natural habitat. Oh, and you'll have the best perspective—from the sea of Old Cockspur Lighthouse, Fort Pulaski and the North Beach of Tybee Island.

CAPTAIN MIKE'S DOLPHIN TOURS
1 Old US Hwy 80 | Tybee Island | 912.786.5848 | tybeedolphins.com

{ COCKSPUR ISLAND LIGHT IS THE SMALLEST LIGHTHOUSE IN GEORGIA }

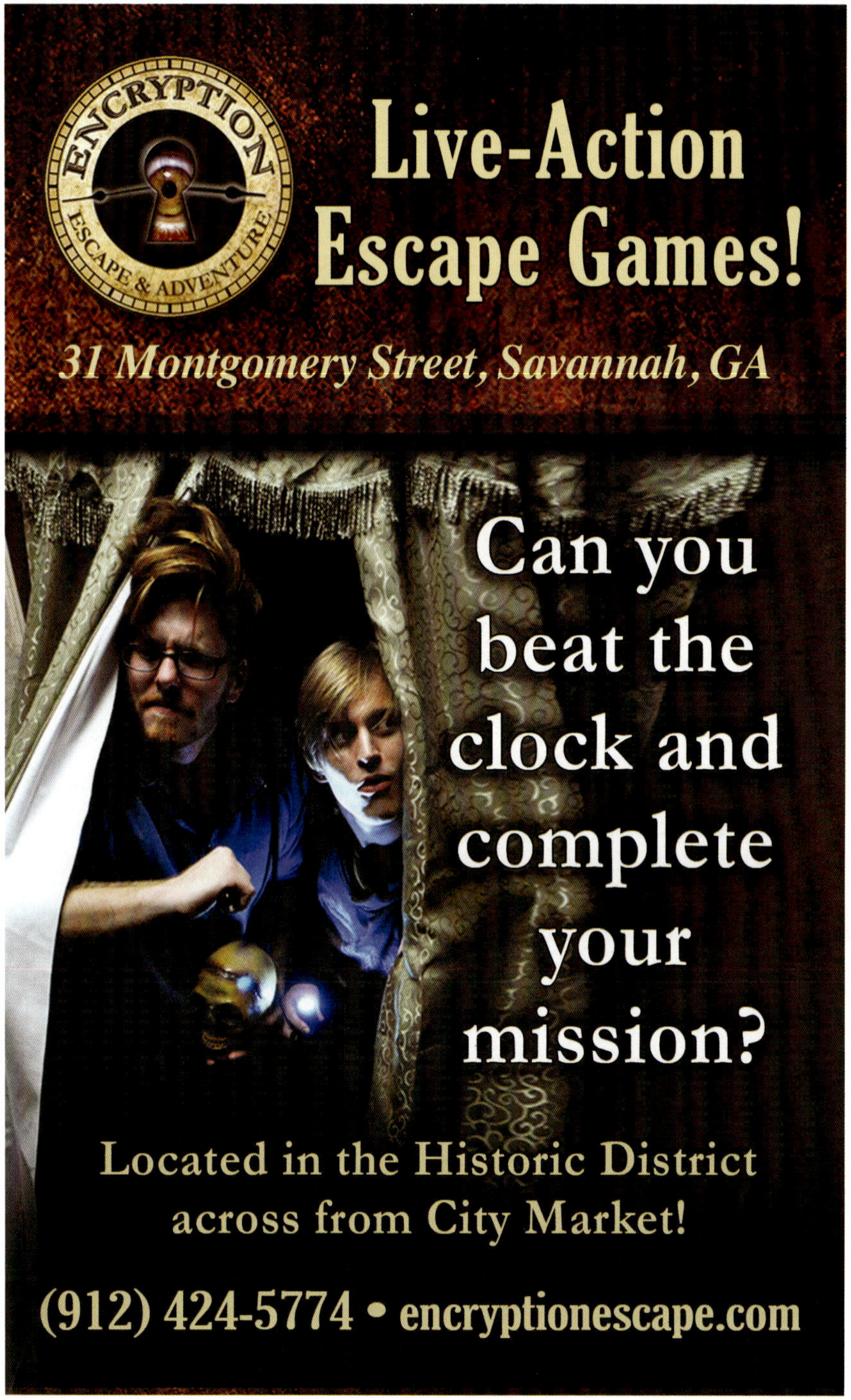

Live-Action Escape Games!

31 Montgomery Street, Savannah, GA

Can you beat the clock and complete your mission?

Located in the Historic District across from City Market!

(912) 424-5774 • encryptionescape.com

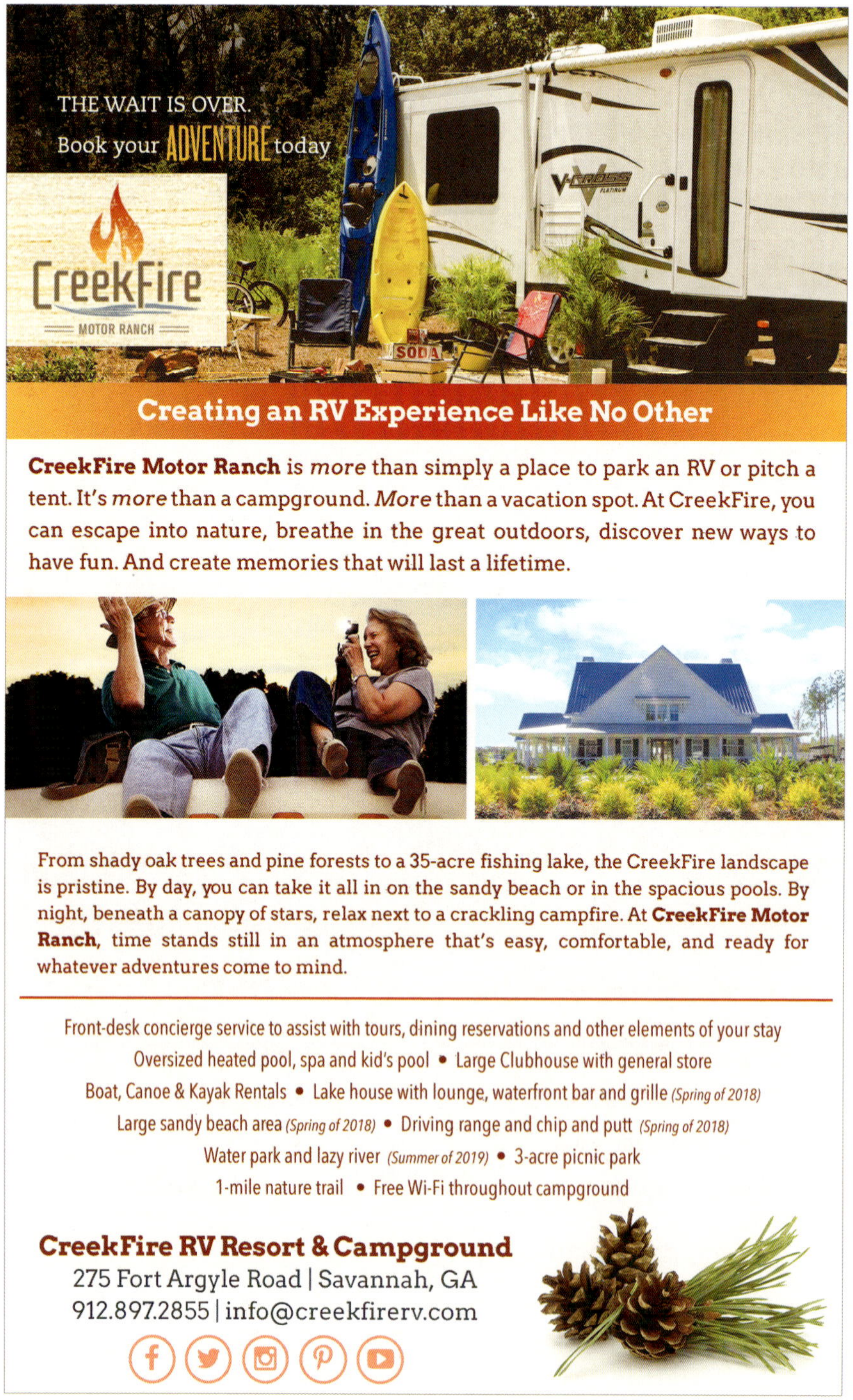

THE WAIT IS OVER.
Book your ADVENTURE today

Creating an RV Experience Like No Other

CreekFire Motor Ranch is *more* than simply a place to park an RV or pitch a tent. It's *more* than a campground. *More* than a vacation spot. At CreekFire, you can escape into nature, breathe in the great outdoors, discover new ways to have fun. And create memories that will last a lifetime.

From shady oak trees and pine forests to a 35-acre fishing lake, the CreekFire landscape is pristine. By day, you can take it all in on the sandy beach or in the spacious pools. By night, beneath a canopy of stars, relax next to a crackling campfire. At **CreekFire Motor Ranch**, time stands still in an atmosphere that's easy, comfortable, and ready for whatever adventures come to mind.

Front-desk concierge service to assist with tours, dining reservations and other elements of your stay
Oversized heated pool, spa and kid's pool • Large Clubhouse with general store
Boat, Canoe & Kayak Rentals • Lake house with lounge, waterfront bar and grille *(Spring of 2018)*
Large sandy beach area *(Spring of 2018)* • Driving range and chip and putt *(Spring of 2018)*
Water park and lazy river *(Summer of 2019)* • 3-acre picnic park
1-mile nature trail • Free Wi-Fi throughout campground

CreekFire RV Resort & Campground
275 Fort Argyle Road | Savannah, GA
912.897.2855 | info@creekfirerv.com

{ FLY IN A HELICOPTER }

Take the ride of your lifetime aboard a small yellow helicopter. Fly low and fast along the Savannah River while you enjoy a unique perspective of downtown Savannah, Old Fort Jackson, Fort Pulaski, Whitemarsh Island, the Cockspur, and Tybee and Hilton Head lighthouses. The views are spectacular!

OLD CITY HELICOPTERS
1125 Bob Harmon Road | 912.247.0047 | oldcityhelicopters.com

{ ESCAPE FROM A LIVE-ACTION ADVENTURE }

If you've got what it takes to solve a mission within 60 minutes using only your wits, then you're ready for live-action escape. You'll enter a high-production value, themed adventure room and while immersed in this new setting, locate clues, crack codes, and solve puzzles to accomplish your assigned mission. You'll have to work together to solve the mystery. Although missions vary, the end goal is always the same, players have just one hour to beat the clock.

ENCRYPTION ESCAPE
31 Montgomery Street | 912.424.5774 | encryptionescape.com

{ RIDE A LOCOMOTIVE }

Thomas the Tank Engine would have felt right at home at the Roundhouse Railroad Museum, where a giant turntable still shifts cars onto tracks. Little engineers can learn about the history of steam engines and belt-driven machinery, and model train buffs will kick up their heels at the huge display of downtown Savannah! The museum is open daily, but train rides are seasonal—call ahead to check the schedule.

COASTAL HISTORICAL SOCIETY - ROUNDHOUSE
655 Louisville Road | 912.651.6823 | chsgeorgia.org/roundhouse

{ GEORGIA STATE RAILROAD MUSEUM OFFERS GUIDED TOURS AND TRAIN RIDES }

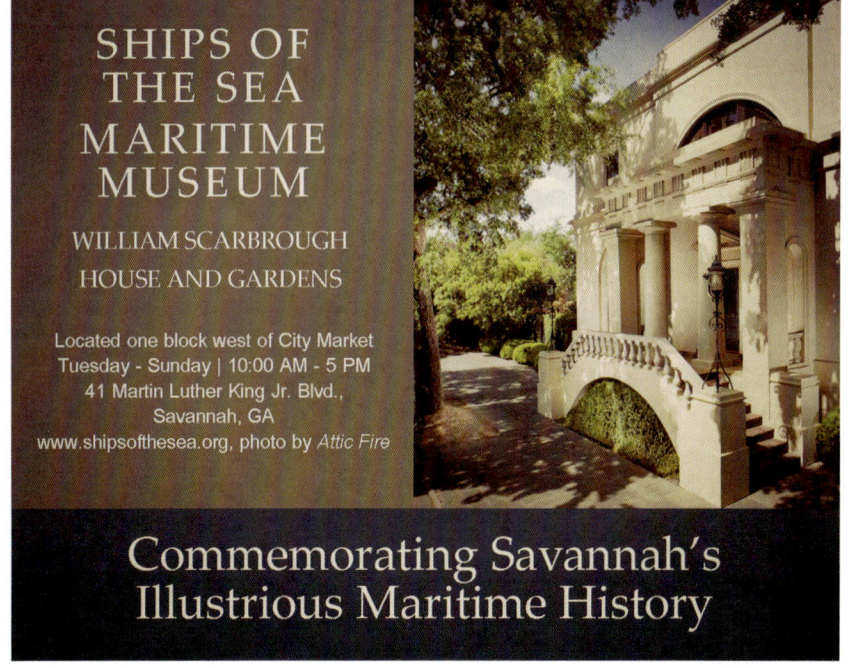

{ CATHEDRAL OF ST. JOHN THE BAPTIST IS FOUND OFF LAFAYETTE SQUARE }

Discover MASSIE HERITAGE CENTER

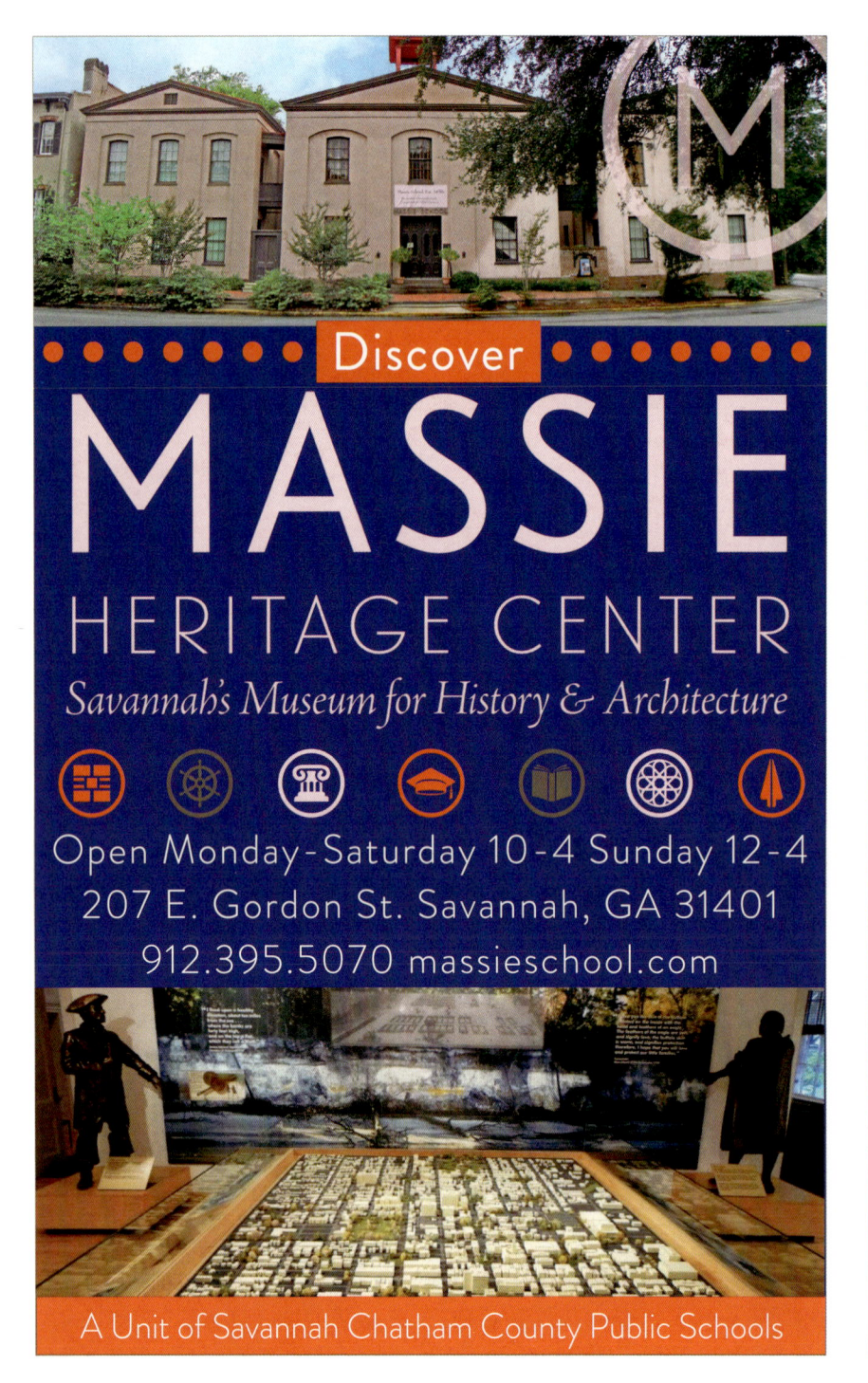

Savannah's Museum for History & Architecture

Open Monday-Saturday 10-4 Sunday 12-4
207 E. Gordon St. Savannah, GA 31401
912.395.5070 massieschool.com

A Unit of Savannah Chatham County Public Schools

SAVANNAH MUSIC FESTIVAL

MARCH 29–APRIL 14, 2018

Tickets: 912.525.5050 | savannahmusicfestival.org

7 Things Savannah Had First

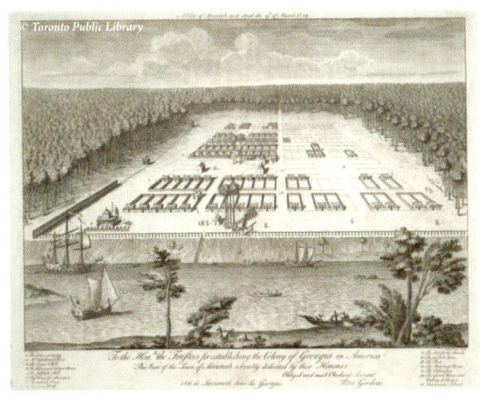   

{ PLANNED CITY }
Savannah was the first city set into a grid pattern with originally 24 squares, trustee lots and more, which was planned by General James Oglethorpe. Twenty-two of these squares remain today and the Historic District is one of the most walkable downtown areas in the country. *(above, first)*

{ LIGHTHOUSE ON SOUTH ATLANTIC COAST }
The first lighthouse to aid navigation in the South was erected near the present Tybee Island Lighthouse.

{ BLACK BAPTIST CONGREGATION IN AMERICA }
The first Black Baptist congregation was organized at Brampton Plantation outside Savannah. Their descendants established Savannah's First African Baptist Church and First Bryan Baptist Church. *(above, second)*

{ GOLF COURSE IN AMERICA }
In 1794, the first golf course in America was established in Savannah. The Savannah Golf Club remains as one of the most prestigious courses in the city.

{ COTTON GIN }
Eli Whitney, a Yale graduate, invented the cotton gin while serving as a tutor on General Nathaniel Greene's Mulberry Grove Plantation outside Savannah. This invention revolutionized the South, making it possible to process cotton on a large scale.

{ ART MUSEUM IN THE SOUTH }
Built in 1819 as a mansion for Alexander Telfair, the Telfair Museum of Art was left to the Georgia Historical Society in 1875. The museum's collection contains works by American and European artists, as well as special exhibits. *(above, third)*

{ GIRL SCOUTS }
On March 12, 1912, at her residence on Lafayette Square, Juliette Gordon Low formed the first Girl Scout troop in America. Low's birthplace, at the corner of Oglethorpe Avenue and Bull Street, is maintained by the Girl Scouts of the U.S.A., and is a museum and national program center. *(above, fourth)*

3 EXCITING WAYS TO EXPERIENCE THE
Great Outdoors in Savannah

© John Alexander Photography

AN INTEGRAL PART OF ANY SAVANNAH VISIT IS GETTING OUTDOORS.

Conservation efforts along the coast have left elements of it pristine and untouched, waiting to be gently explored. Pack up your backpack and get your gear ready to enjoy Savannah's unforgettable coastal environment.

Visit Oatland Island, located just minutes from downtown to get up close & personal with nature.

{ SPOT WILDLIFE }
AT THE OATLAND ISLAND WILDLIFE CENTER

Get in touch with Savannah's wild side by walking the trails of this local conservation center. Stop at exhibits along the way to see wolves, deer, birds of prey, alligators, foxes, bobcats, cougars, tortoises and more, while learning about the impact the animals have on the area.

{ FIND ADVENTURE }
ON A KAYAKING ECO-TOUR

Several kayaking companies in Savannah and on Tybee Island offer a variety of eco-tour excursions that feature marshland, Little Tybee Island, Cockspur Lighthouse, a bird sanctuary and more.

{ CAMP OUT }
ON LITTLE TYBEE ISLAND

This wilderness gem showcases rich, coastal salt marshes, pristine beaches, natural dunes and subtropical forests of live oak, pine and palm. Spend a night or two camping out on Little Tybee Island, only reachable by charter boat or kayak/paddleboard, for a chance to spot wildlife including the egret, heron, white ibis and the endangered woodstork as well as the roseate spoonbill, osprey and bald eagle.

{ THE ORIGINAL TYBEE PIER WAS BUILT BY THE CENTRAL GEORGIA RAILROAD IN THE 1890S }

Visit TYBEE ISLAND

Pronounced Tie-Bee

Just 20 minutes east of the city, you'll discover a great escape that is best experienced barefoot – Tybee Island, Georgia. Unlike many coastal beaches, which are dotted with high-rise condominiums and theme parks, the people of Tybee Island have made it their mission to retain the island's vintage charm, providing a truly laid-back year-round vacation experience. *Welcome to Tybee Time!*

With a history that dates back to the eighteenth century, complete with lore of pirates and buried treasure, Tybee's five miles of sandy public beaches officially became a resort destination in 1887. At that time, Savannah's wealthy would visit the island, known as the community of "Ocean City," arriving by train or by steamship. Fast forward 130 years and Tybee's palm-lined highway, which remains the island's sole access route to this day, makes it easy for beach-goers to bask in the warmth of the Southern sun.

Once you arrive on the island, if your idea of the perfect beach day includes planting a chair in the sand for hours on end, Tybee offers ample opportunity to do just that. You can opt for a quiet secluded stretch of beach on the north side of the island, or the daily attractions near the scenic Tybee Island Pier on the south side. For those who prefer a more active experience, Tybee also offers dolphin tours, deep-sea fishing excursions, kiteboarding lessons, kayaking, jet skiing, paddle boarding and more.

Another must-see while visiting Tybee is the Tybee Island Light Station. Built in 1773, the Tybee lighthouse is the oldest and tallest in Georgia. Climb the lighthouse's 178 steps and you will experience a breathtaking birds-eye view from atop the lighthouse.

As you set foot on Tybee you're sure to notice that both Southern charm and a commitment to preservation run deep on the island. From renovated vintage beach cottages to the newly-restored historic Tybee Post Theater, the island continues to be the perfect complement to Savannah.

Without a doubt, as you feel the sand between your toes and hear the crash of the waves, looking out over a horizon that stretches as far as the eye can see, you, too, will be swept up in the authentic beach town of Tybee. *All we can say is, join the club!*

TO LEARN MORE ABOUT TYBEE ISLAND AND PLAN YOUR BEACH VACATION, VISIT **VISITTYBEE.COM**

Savannah's *Sandy Shore* is a barrier island and small city known for its *lush & sandy* beaches.

savannah: a southern journey | 35

{ IN GEORGIA, MORE THAN $8 MILLION WORTH OF SHRIMP ARE HARVESTED EVERY YEAR }

VISIT TYBEE

Wake up to the waves. Savor it all. Leave the rest behind.
A 20-minute drive is all it takes.
VisitTybee.com

Visit Tybee Island
SAVANNAH'S BEACH

{ THE PORT OF SAVANNAH IS THE LARGEST SINGLE CONTAINER TERMINAL IN NORTH AMERICA }

Where the tide

is the only time that matters.

Golden Isles
GEORGIA

St. Simons Island · Sea Island · Jekyll Island · Little St. Simons Island · Brunswick

Goldenisles.com | (800) 933-2627

The Golden Isles is conveniently located just over an hour south of Savannah.

Welcome to the
GOLDEN ISLES

Along the Georgia coast lies a stretch of land that is like no other. Here you will find centuries-old oak trees draped with Spanish moss that line the streets and meet miles of sun-drenched beaches. Vast marshlands, winding rivers, plentiful nature and wildlife beckon visitors who return for generations. The destination is reminiscent of a bygone era as historic landmarks can be found around every bend. This is perhaps the best kept secret on the East Coast; this is the Golden Isles.

Conveniently located just over an hour south of Savannah, the Golden Isles is comprised of four unique barrier islands: St. Simons Island, Sea Island, Little St. Simons Island and Jekyll Island, each with its own charisma and personality for you to discover, and all are complemented by the mainland port city, Brunswick. This distinct quality landed the Golden Isles on Travel + Leisure's list of World's Best Islands in the Continental U.S. and Canada for three consecutive years.

ST. SIMONS ISLAND

The largest of the Golden Isles, St. Simons Island (voted both "America's Most Romantic Town" and "Favorite Beach Town" by *Travel + Leisure*) features hundreds of quality dining and shopping options to please any taste. The picture-perfect barrier island is filled with exceptional historic sites, museums, plantation-era ruins and a National Historic Monument. Uncover an array of island activities, including kayaking, fishing, paddle boarding, biking and golf, as well as accommodations that fit any budget.

SEA ISLAND

An internationally acclaimed resort, Sea Island is the only resort in the world to have received four *Forbes* Five-Star awards for nine consecutive years. The resort offers unmatched amenities, world class golf and all of the activities under the sun, from a yacht club to a shooting school to a 65,000-square-foot award-winning spa. For those seeking the most intimate and luxurious experience, Sea Island has it all.

"Each of the four enchanting barrier islands and the mainland city have their own charisma & personality to discover."

LITTLE ST. SIMONS ISLAND

Prized for its pristine beauty, gracious hospitality and secluded worlds-away appeal, Little St. Simons Island has retained the charm and unhurried pace of coastal living and features gracious accommodations for only thirty-two overnight guests. The island is a paradise for nature lovers and offers a host of naturalist-led experiences on its seven miles of secluded beaches and over 11,000 acres of undeveloped wilderness.

JEKYLL ISLAND

The southernmost island, Jekyll Island, offers ten miles of beaches, more than twenty miles of bike paths, a National Historic Landmark District, the Georgia Sea Turtle Center and coastal dining options to suit any palate. The island is perfect for welcoming families with a variety of shops, coastal activities and spacious accommodations.

BRUNSWICK

Venture into the city of Brunswick to discover history as rich as its seafood. From the unique signature squares of Brunswick to the famous Historic Ritz Theatre, find architecture dating back to the early 1800s. With shrimp boats heading out from the docks daily, there is always plenty of fresh, local seafood to be had-and don't miss our namesake dish, Brunswick Stew!

Rich in history and culture, along with laidback towns and unparalleled beauty, the Golden Isles experience is one of the richest along the Atlantic seaboard. Every season shines with activities and new experiences: art and antique shows, festivals, food and wine events, historic celebrations, performing arts and more. To learn more about the Golden Isles and to plan your trip, visit GoldenIsles.com.

TO LEARN MORE AND PLAN A TRIP TO THE GOLDEN ISLES, VISIT **GOLDENISLES.COM**

The Golden Isles plays host to a range of can't-miss events throughout the year, perfect for families, foodies and festival-goers of all kinds.

SPRING

Georgia Elvis Festival
Brunswick

80th Annual Blessing of the Fleet
Brunswick

Turtle Crawl Triathlon & Nest Fest
Jekyll Island

SUMMER

Georgia Sea Island Festival
St. Simons Island

4th of July Celebrations
Golden Isles

FALL

Shrimp & Grits Festival
Jekyll Island

Brunswick Rockin' Stewbilee
Brunswick

St. Simons Island Food + Spirits Festival
St. Simons Island

RSM Classic
Sea Island

WINTER

Tree Lighting Festival & Holidays in History
Jekyll Island

Brunswick Christmas Parade
Brunswick

Island Treasures
Jekyll Island

{ THE GREAT EGRET LIVES ALONG GEORGIA'S COAST YEAR-ROUND }

Where your vacation becomes a

Lifestyle

HiltonHeadIsland.org

HILTON HEAD ISLAND
South Carolina

Just over the bridge from Savannah, you'll enter a world where nature's beauty and resort luxuries coexist like nowhere else on earth. On Hilton Head Island, rich Gullah Heritage, born of a culture more than two centuries old, is yours to explore. Dine, shop, renew your sense of inner peace and still make it back to your room in time for turndown service. As long as you promise next time, you'll stay a little longer.

HILTONHEADISLAND.ORG | 800-523-3373 | @VISITHILTONHEAD | @HILTONHEADSC | VISITHILTONHEAD | HILTONHEADSC

South Carolina Just right.

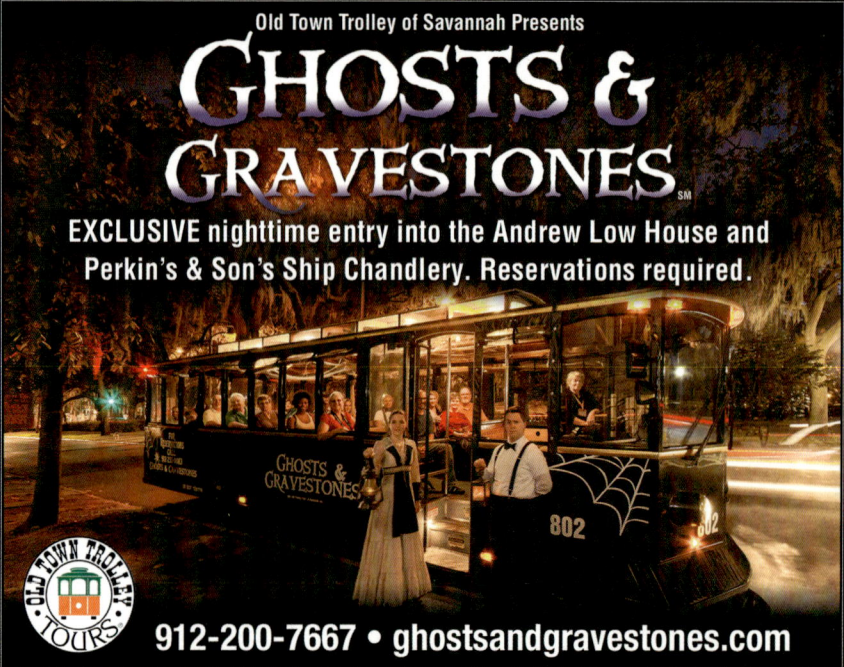

Savannah's Scary Side

ESTABLISHED IN 1733, SAVANNAH HAS A LONG, VIBRANT HISTORY. AND WITH THIS HISTORY COMES YEARS OF HAUNTINGS, STORIES OF WHICH ARE WELL KNOWN THROUGHOUT THE CITY TODAY.

{ THE PIRATES' HOUSE }

Underneath this famed restaurant are the remains of one of the oldest buildings in Savannah. The deeper you go, the creepier it becomes with tunnels that run from the basement to the Savannah River, where many a sailor met his fate at the hands of

{ MADISON SQUARE }

During the American Revolutionary War, the Battle of Savannah was fought in the area known as Madison Square. Shadowy figures are said to roam this square and many believe them to be soldiers who were slain on this very ground.

{ RIVER STREET }

This retail and restaurant mecca was once home to warehouses and ship docks dating back to the very founding of Savannah. With a history like that, there's bound to be a lingering ghost or two peering out on the cobblestone streets.

Savannah 16

Atlanta ⇄ Savannah

✓ Daily Express Non-stop Departures
✓ First Class Shuttle Transportation
✓ Onboard Entertainment
✓ Complimentary Refreshments
✓ Free Wi-Fi and Power Outlets

WWW.SAVANNAH16.COM
Customer Service: 404.500.3966

SAVANNAH RIVERBOAT CRUISES

Experience Historic Savannah

- Narrated Harbor Sightseeing Cruise
- Narrated Harbor Luncheon Cruise
- Sunset Cruise
- Sunday Brunch Cruise
- Dinner Entertainment Cruise
- Monday Gospel Dinner Cruise
- Moonlight Party Cruise

FOR RESERVATIONS & TICKETS
Visit www.savannahriverboat.com
or call 912.232.6404

Savannah Riverboat Cruises
9 East River Street
Savannah, GA 31401
Departing from River Street behind City Hall

Let us host your wedding, corporate party or special event!

savannah: a southern journey | 45

GETTING AROUND
Savannah

Whether you arrived via jet plane at Savannah-Hilton Head International Airport, rolled in on the highway or sailed in by boat, we extend our warmest welcome. As nice as your hotel room may be, you didn't come to Savannah to spend your whole time in there, right? So, let's get you out the door and on your way to exploring the remarkable scenery and sights of Savannah.

SAVANNAH IS REGULARLY NAMED ONE OF THE BEST WALKING CITIES IN AMERICA, AND YOU ONLY NEED TO STROLL FOR A COUPLE OF YARDS TO FIGURE OUT WHY—IT'S FLAT, MOSTLY SHADY AND THERE'S ALWAYS SOMETHING TO SEE.

It's totally possible—and incredibly fascinating—to spend days strolling through the nation's largest Landmark Historic District. But with so much here to see and do, your feet might have different plans. Check out some other ways to see Savannah in style.

{ BY FARE-FREE TRANSPORTATION }

Look for the plum-colored logo on buses and signs for fare-free transportation, in and around Savannah's beautiful Historic District. The dot gets you where you want to go, when you need to get there. You can also ride what the locals call the "CAT"—Chatham Area Transit. The CAT offers bike sharing, bus, paratransit, and ferry services throughout Chatham County.

{ BY WHEEL }

Prefer people-powered transportation? The three wheeled buggies of Savannah's pedi-cabs accommodate two people at a time for a breezy jaunt. Part bike, part modern rickshaw, these environmentally responsible vehicles are a favorite among bar-hoppers. The pedal pushers are happy to take you a few blocks or on a thorough tour down to Forsyth Park.

{ BY ROAD }

It's always helpful to engage the services of a seasoned tour guide. For an open-air ride that hits all the important historical points from downtown through the historic district, a trolley is the way to go. Each has its own starting point and convenient parking lot and offers general Savannah tours as well as ghost tours, pirate tours, beach excursions and specialty services. Rest assured, there are so many stories in this city; surprises will await you at every turn!

{ BY ANY MEANS NECESSARY }

Looking for alternative transportation? You can tour Savannah by Segway, Vespa, rented Cadillac, horse-drawn carriage or even helicopter.

CAT
CHATHAM AREA TRANSIT

CATCH A CAT

catchacat.org

(912) 233-5767 • catchacat.org

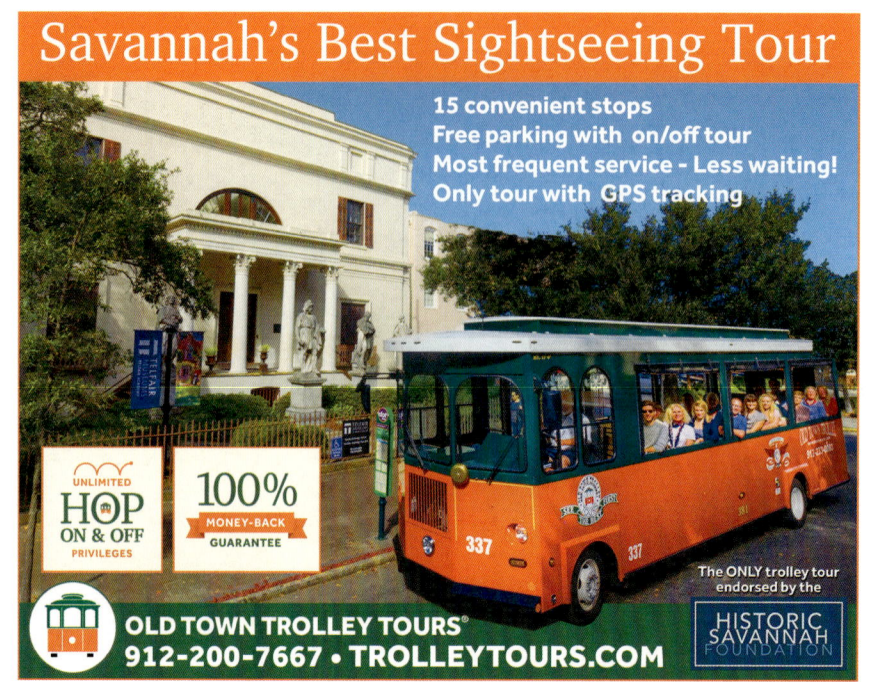

Savannah's Best Sightseeing Tour

- 15 convenient stops
- Free parking with on/off tour
- Most frequent service - Less waiting!
- Only tour with GPS tracking

UNLIMITED HOP ON & OFF PRIVILEGES

100% MONEY-BACK GUARANTEE

OLD TOWN TROLLEY TOURS
912-200-7667 • TROLLEYTOURS.COM

The ONLY trolley tour endorsed by the HISTORIC SAVANNAH FOUNDATION

---

nour·ish
NATURAL BATH PRODUCTS

HANDMADE in savannah

Glycerin Soap • Bath Fizzies • Salt Scrubs
Handmade Natural Soap • Soy Candles

no parabens • no mineral oil • no phenoxyethanol • no phthalates

Downtown Savannah • 202 West Broughton St. • 912.232.3213
Midtown Savannah • 5501 Abercorn St. • 912.777.5479

nourishsavannah.com

Rent a Vespa
MOTORINI
912.201.1899

11 West Duffy Street
Savannah, GA 31401

vespasavannah.com

savannah: a southern journey | 49

City Market is a place where the past & present *beautifully combine* to create a must-see Savannah attraction.

CITY MARKET

WHERE CITY *Activity* MEETS LOCAL *Creativity*

{ DISCOVER CITY MARKET }

Within this unique marketplace there is always something new to encounter, something different to find and something hidden to uncover. You may have to look around a corner, behind a door or up a remote staircase, but that's part of the charm that makes City Market so special.

Since the early 1700s, City Market has been the commercial and social center of historic Savannah. Located on the original site of the market used by farmers and traders of all kinds to sell their goods and wares, City Market offers the best of what is old and new in Savannah.

Today, Savannah's City Market comprises a four-block area of restored warehouses and shop fronts adjacent to Ellis Square. This charming, open-air marketplace houses a wealth of things to do, whether you come for the entertainment, to shop, dine or just relax a moment and rest your weary feet.

CITY MARKET
The Art & Soul of Savannah

{ FIND SOMETHING BEAUTIFUL }

Savannah boasts a vibrant art scene and City Market is at the center of it all. As you visit City Market, allow plenty of time to enjoy the wide variety of art galleries – from fine art to contemporary art – featuring more than 50 local artists. An especially unique experience offered at City Market is the Art Center, where you can watch artists create original works in their studios.

{ FIND SOMETHING TO TAKE HOME }

The mercantile and produce offerings of yesteryear in City Market have been replaced by an eclectic blend of art galleries and specialty shops. Shoppers will discover unique gifts, original works of art, freshly made candy and a host of other delights at the many shops and boutiques that welcome visitors to browse and buy.

{ CITY MARKET OFFERS THE BEST OF WHAT IS OLD AND NEW IN SAVANNAH }

City Market offers a one-of-a-kind experience in a one-of-a-kind place.

{ BE ENTERTAINED }

Entertainment in Savannah abounds, and City Market is certainly a hub for fun things to do. Outdoor entertainment, including street musicians, live music and special events, is featured in the pedestrian-only courtyards of City Market almost daily throughout the year. As the evening nears, City Market's tucked-away nightspots offer a variety of enticing cocktails to cap off a spirited night on the town. Whether on the rooftop or on the lower level of the courtyard, you're sure to find a place that suits your preference. Additionally, carriage and trolley tours leave and return to City Market each day making it the perfect embarkation point to explore more of our beautiful city.

{ FILL YOUR BELLY }

City Market is also home to some of the best places to eat in Savannah. Diners can satisfy their appetites at one of the many restaurants, cafes or specialty food shops located within steps of one another. The options will appeal to all tastes and pocketbooks with a casual atmosphere and outdoor dining that are available just about year 'round. If a sit-down meal isn't on the menu, you can still sample City Market's best by simply enjoying an ice cream, espresso or cocktail in the public courtyard while watching people pass by.

Though the farmers and merchants from centuries past may have never envisioned the City Market of today, it is their entrepreneurial spirit that has enlivened this unique place into the bustling epicenter of activity that it has become. Without a doubt, City Market offers visitors a one-of-a-kind experience in a one-of-a-kind place where past and present beautifully combine to create a truly local must-see Savannah attraction.

EXPERIENCE CITY MARKET

City Market is not a place you visit. *It's a place you discover and explore.* A place that's **romantic, historic, serene** and **exciting**. You may have to look around a corner, behind an old door or up a remote staircase. But that's just part of the charm and what makes City Market so special.

CITY MARKET
The Art & Soul of Savannah

912.232.4903 • SavannahCityMarket.com
Jefferson at West St. Julian Street

ART CENTER
SAVANNAH

A community of 35 working artists who make and sell their work in a series of studio lofts and galleries.

It's a Beautiful Day to Explore Savannah!

Hop the free ferry from the City Hall Landing for an authentic Savannah experience. Just across from River Street you'll find the finest coastal cuisine and stunning views of downtown at Aqua Star Seafood Kitchen—don't miss our famous Sunday Jazz Brunch! Enjoy cold beer, tasty burgers and Savannah's "Best Golf Course" at The Club at Savannah Harbor. Refresh both body and mind with a signature massage at the Heavenly Spa by Westin. Low country luxury awaits on Hutchinson Island.

Heavenly Spa
heavenlyspasavannah.com
912.201.2250

The Club at Savannah Harbor
theclubatsavannahharbor.com
912.201.2250

Aqua Star Seafood Kitchen
aquastarseafoodkitchen.com
912.201.2250

Finding Romance in Savannah

It is hard to imagine a destination more romantic than Savannah.

Lacy curtains of moss drape ancient oaks. Flowers bloom throughout the seasons, sending out delicate fragrance. The evening air is sultry, occasionally ruffling one's hair with a breeze off the river. An empty bench for two seems to beckon, eager to serve as the setting for a first kiss—or an embrace celebrating a lifetime of love.

Dream Weddings find their way into reality here, as Savannah has been named one of America's *Most Romantic Cities.*

58 | savannah: a southern journey

Savannah has long enjoyed her reputation as one of America's most romantic cities and has indeed become one of the most popular wedding destinations in the world. Dream weddings find their way into reality here with a thriving industry of professionals specifically catering to the couple's vision of their perfect day—be it exchanging vows in a gazebo on the square before being whisked away in a horse-drawn carriage or declaring their eternal love while barefoot on the beach.

Honeymoons, anniversaries or just-for-fun jaunts are also excellent reasons to share Savannah with your favorite person. Enjoy each other's company as you spend the days exploring shops and museums then wile away the nights at world-class restaurants and cozy pubs.

Walk in the footsteps of so many contented couples that have come before. After all, what more fortuitous a place to cultivate a long and happy romance than a place that's stood the test of time.

savannah: a southern journey | 59

TOP 10 REASONS YOU NEED TO MAKE YOUR WAY TO

River Street

This cobblestoned stretch is a favorite place to pick up a perfect piece to remember Savannah, enjoy a sumptuous meal, watch a taffy pull or hop on a trolley ride to explore more than 100 shops, restaurants and pubs.

HERE'S A HOST OF FACTS ABOUT SAVANNAH'S RIVERFRONT YOU MAY NOT KNOW.

IT'S A MULTICULTURAL WONDERLAND

Throughout the year, River Street hosts family-friendly festivals from Oktoberfest, featuring lederhosen and wiener dog races, to Blues, Jazz & BBQ with its tasty treats and sultry sounds. And of course, there's the largest St. Patrick's Day celebration in the country, when everyone becomes Irish for the day just for showing up.

YOU CAN SIT WITH HISTORY — LITERALLY

Nestled above the river level on Yamacraw Bluff on the property of the Hyatt Regency Savannah is a Mediterranean-style rounded white bench created by the Colonial Dames in 1905. The bench marks the exact spot General Oglethorpe pitched his tent to rest his first night after docking in the new colony on February 12, 1733.

THE BEST VIEWS OF RIVER STREET ARE FROM THE RIVER

The beloved Savannah Belles Ferry system offers a unique link between downtown Savannah and Hutchinson Island. This free ride across the Savannah River will get you up close and personal with the big cargo ships that pass by. You can also check out some other fare free transportation at connectonthedot.com.

THE NATION'S FOURTH-BUSIEST CONTAINER PORT LIES JUST UP THE RIVER

The Georgia Ports Authority handles millions of shipping containers from all over the world, and many of the goods that hit everyone's favorite stores around the country passed through Savannah first. You surely won't miss a ship passing by because this port is the busiest port on the East Coast.

IT'S MUSIC TO YOUR EARS

When you stroll down River Street at night, chances are, you'll hear live music coming from some of the bars and restaurants. You may even see some street performers! At most of the festivals that call River Street home, you'll find local bands that range from Southern rock to smooth jazz. With a built-in, open-air stage, you're sure to find your sound.

THE ENDS OF THE EARTH ARE UNDER YOUR FEET

Savannah's early developers recycled the ballast used on ships to pave the streets, laying cobblestones originally quarried in Canada, the British Isles, France, Spain and beyond. Still solid—and charming—after almost three centuries, the varied materials of River Street (as well as some of the retaining walls and structures) include limestone, granite, quartz and basalt.

A FAMOUS GIRL WAVES YOU CLOSER

Look closely for the statue. Do you see her? That's Florence Martus also known as "the Waving Girl." She took it upon herself to be the unofficial greeter of all ships that entered and left the Port of Savannah between 1887 and 1931. Her undying spirit lives on with everyone who will greet you along the way.

PIRATES ONCE DOCKED ON THESE SHORES

Lore has it that sea-faring outcasts and plunderers—including the fearsome Bluebeard—made liberal use of Savannah's old inns and pubs in the 18th and 19th centuries. The old tunnel at the Pirate's House Restaurant emptied out near the river, where unsuspecting sailors plied with rum were shanghaied onto waiting vessels and forced into pirate life.

DOCKING DIDN'T COME EASY

The high bluff made for good anchorage for early ships, but the steep bank and treacherous currents proved challenging for loading and unloading passengers and supplies in the city's early days. Savannah's wharves benefitted from the Industrial Revolution when equipment powerful enough to drive concrete piles into the river bottom was brought in, creating easy access for large vessels. You can still see the public wharf towards the east end, constructed in 1872 for smaller boats.

SHOPPING HASN'T CHANGED MUCH IN A FEW HUNDRED YEARS

You can peruse the wares of more than a hundred merchants up and down River Street, just like Savannah shoppers did when the road was little more than a bumpy route. Shopping options range from artisan wares to delicious confections.

RIVER STREET LIQUOR

WELCOME TO THE SMALLEST LIQUOR STORE IN THE WORLD.

ONCE UPON A TIME, A MAN WALKED INTO A VERY SMALL ROOM AND SAID, "THIS SHOULD BE A LIQUOR STORE!" THE END

@RSLSAVANNAH

LOCATED AT THE FAR EAST END OF RIVER STREET, OUR ECLECTIC STORE CARRIES YOUR FAVORITE BRANDS, ALONG WITH LOCAL FLARES. WE'RE PERFECT FOR VISITORS STAYING IN OUR BEAUTIFUL CITY, BUT ALSO STRIVE TO SERVE OUR LOCAL COMMUNITY. OUR PASSION AND DETERMINATION SHOWS WITH IMMENSE CARE OF INDIVIDUAL CUSTOMERS AND THEIR NEEDS. WE'RE ALSO THE ONLY PACKAGE SHOP OPEN ON SUNDAY.

COME PARTY WITH RIVER STREET LIQUOR!

River Street Liquor
SPIRITS, BEER & WINE

RIVERSTREETLIQUOR.COM | INFO@RIVERSTREETLIQUOR.COM | CALL US: 912.944.4449 | 425 E. RIVER STREET | SAVANNAH, GA 31401 | OPEN: MON-SAT: 10:00 AM - 11:45 PM / SUN: 12:30 PM - 11:30 PM

IT HAS ALWAYS BEEN MY RULE NEVER TO SMOKE WHEN ASLEEP, AND NEVER TO REFRAIN WHEN AWAKE.

~ MARK TWAIN ~

River Street Liquor
SPIRITS, BEER & WINE

RIVERSTREETLIQUOR.COM | INFO@RIVERSTREETLIQUOR.COM | CALL US: 912.944.4449 | 425 E. RIVER STREET | SAVANNAH, GA 31401 | OPEN: MON-SAT: 10:00 AM - 11:45 PM / SUN: 12:30 PM - 11:30 PM

BELFORD'S

SAVANNAH

SEAFOOD AND STEAKS

Belford's Savannah Seafood & Steaks

Casual Fine Dining in City Market
315 West St. Julian Street
912.233.2626 • www.belfordssavannah.com

Private Dining Available
ACCOMMODATES UP TO 36 GUESTS

| *French cuisine with a modern twist* |

Happy Hour
EVERYDAY! 5 - 7PM

WWW.39RUEDEJEANSAV.COM **39 RUE DE JEAN**

605 W. OGLETHORPE AVE. SAVANNAH, GA • 912.721.0595

Whether *seafood or international plates* inspired by local flavor, you're sure to fill your belly!

COASTAL CUISINE
for the Foodie in You

THE RESTAURANT SCENE IS AS DIVERSE AND STORIED AS THE CITY ITSELF. WHEN IT COMES TO DINING IN SAVANNAH, BRING YOUR APPETITE, BECAUSE YOU OWE IT TO YOURSELF TO TASTE IT ALL.

There's no doubt that Savannah's food scene has an endless array of mouthwatering temptations to please all appetites. From fine-dining establishments tailored to a romantic evening for two to the region's best down-home comfort food and – of course – fresh-caught, straight-from-the-ocean seafood.

Seafood is as much a part of Savannah as cobblestones, squares and Spanish moss. It is the official fare of locals and visitors alike and other than a handful of specialty restaurants, you will be hard pressed to find an establishment in town that doesn't have something seafood on the menu. So, let's get you started with how to order something local!

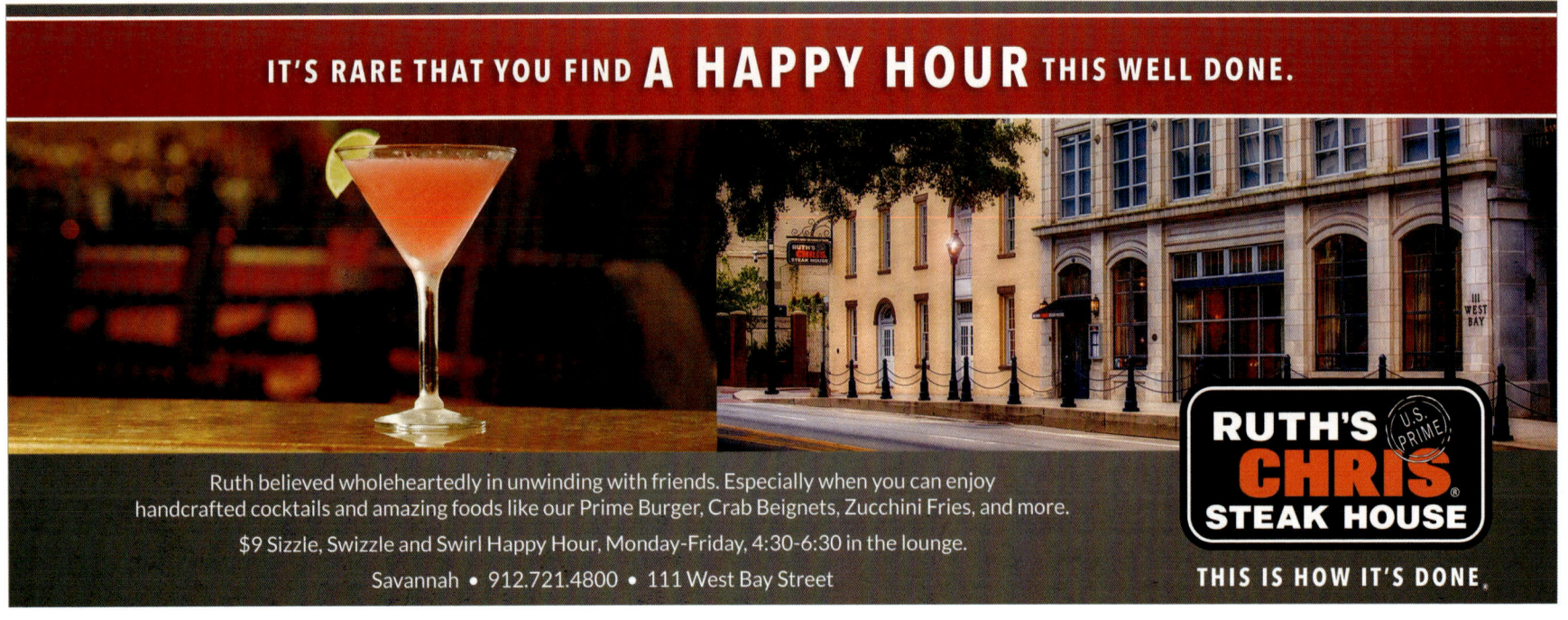

THE PAULA DEEN TOUR

OLD TOWN TROLLEY EXCLUSIVE TOUR

Get Exclusive Access to Paula Deen's Lady & Sons Restaurant only on Old Town Trolley Tours. VIP Preferred Seating: No Lines or Waiting!

Enjoy a narrated history of Paula Deen through the Savannah Historic & Victorian Districts.

912-200-7667 • trolleytours.com

IT'S RARE THAT YOU FIND A HAPPY HOUR THIS WELL DONE.

Ruth believed wholeheartedly in unwinding with friends. Especially when you can enjoy handcrafted cocktails and amazing foods like our Prime Burger, Crab Beignets, Zucchini Fries, and more.

$9 Sizzle, Swizzle and Swirl Happy Hour, Monday-Friday, 4:30-6:30 in the lounge.

Savannah • 912.721.4800 • 111 West Bay Street

RUTH'S CHRIS STEAK HOUSE
U.S. PRIME
THIS IS HOW IT'S DONE.

{ LOW COUNTRY BOIL }

A dish heralding from our Gullah culture, the Lowcountry Boil is one of our favorites. The season's bounty boils in one pot and you pick, peel and eat with your hands. It's delicious. Try it at **Barracuda Bob's Bar & Grill** off of River Street.

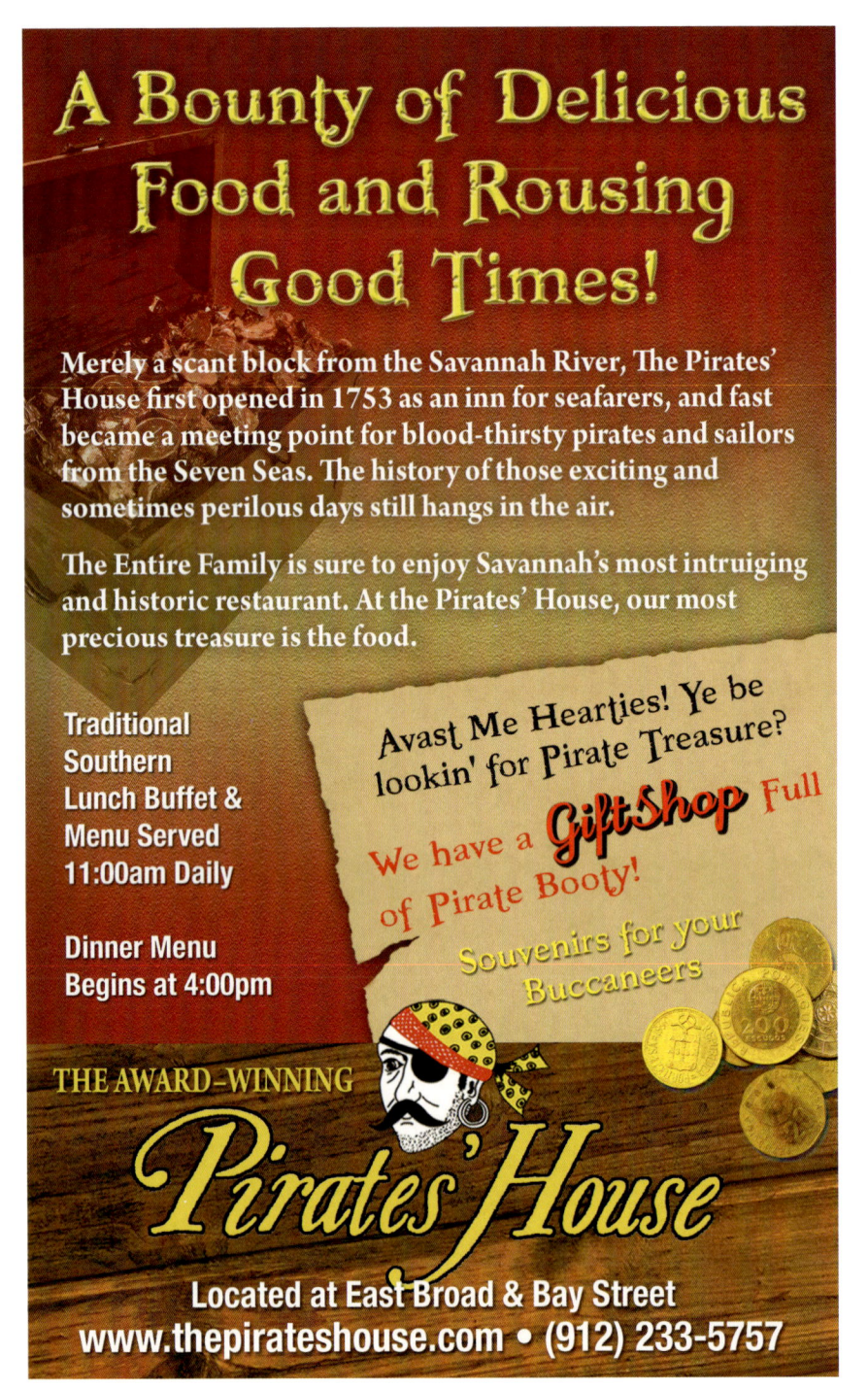

A Bounty of Delicious Food and Rousing Good Times!

Merely a scant block from the Savannah River, The Pirates' House first opened in 1753 as an inn for seafarers, and fast became a meeting point for blood-thirsty pirates and sailors from the Seven Seas. The history of those exciting and sometimes perilous days still hangs in the air.

The Entire Family is sure to enjoy Savannah's most intruiging and historic restaurant. At the Pirates' House, our most precious treasure is the food.

Traditional Southern Lunch Buffet & Menu Served 11:00am Daily

Dinner Menu Begins at 4:00pm

Avast Me Hearties! Ye be lookin' for Pirate Treasure? We have a *GiftShop* Full of Pirate Booty!

Souvenirs for your Buccaneers

THE AWARD-WINNING Pirates' House

Located at East Broad & Bay Street
www.thepirateshouse.com • (912) 233-5757

© John Alexander Photography

{ BOUILLABAISSE }

You can elevate that Lowcountry Boil into a French fish soup, something more suited to a fine-dining date night. The best bouillabaisse in town is found at **39 Rue de Jean**. They create a masterpiece for your mouth with local seafood and a white wine-saffron tomato broth. C'est manifique!

{ SHRIMP & GRITS }

Nothing says Savannah like freshly-caught Georgia shrimp and locally-grown grits—put them together for the perfect pair. You can find the pairing on most menus in town, but it's the variations we love to celebrate. At **Belford's Savannah Seafood and Steaks**, they add another Southern staple—greens. In a mouth-watering, three-part harmony, you'll find this simply southern shrimp, grits and greens in a chardonnay butter sauce with heirloom tomatoes.

{ SHE CRAB SOUP }

The Atlantic Blue Crab is the main ingredient in this creamy soup—also a Savannah staple dish. It doesn't matter if it's hot or cold outside, this rich soup will give you that downhome feel. And, there's a reason that it's the first on the menu at the famed **Pirates' House** restaurant. They've been making this southern tradition for a long time.

{ OYSTERS }

Sweet Savannah oysters are known for their intense salty flavor. From brackish shallow beds off the coast, oysterman harvest from October to May. Whether you prefer them raw, steamed, baked or fried, this coastal delicacy is sure to delight.

BARRACUDA BOB'S BAR & GRILL
SAVANNAH, GA

CONTEMPORARY AMERICAN CASUAL RESTAURANT
- ON RIVER STREET -

SEAFOOD
STEAKS
SANDWICHES
BURGERS
SALADS
PASTAS

100+ CRAFT BEERS

OPEN 7 DAYS A WEEK FOR LUNCH AND DINNER

912-777-4381

19 EAST RIVER STREET
HALF BLOCK EAST OF THE HYATT

912.236.7122 | www.17hundred90.com
307 East President Street

Dinner Nightly
5pm - 9pm

Tavern Daily
3pm UNTIL

{ FISH FROM THE SEA }

Grouper and flounder are found in abundance in Savannah's waters and their mild flavor and flaky white texture make them popular choices in most every restaurant. And, if you're looking for something fresh, try the Carolina Red Trout at **17hundred90**. They pan-sear to perfection and top with the season's sides.

SAVANNAH'S HOME FOR HOT WINGS, COLD BEER AND GOOD TIMES!

WILD WING Cafe

LIVE MUSIC ALL WEEK LONG

33 MADE FROM SCRATCH SAUCES

ICE COLD CRAFT AND LOCAL BEER

FROM THE BEST WINGS SOUTH OF BUFFALO™ AND HAND BREADED NUGGETS IN 33 MADE FROM SCRATCH SAUCES TO BIG GRASS FED 100% ANGUS BURGERS, DELICIOUS SANDWICHES AND CRISP TASTY SALADS, WE'VE GOT JUST THE THING TO MAKE YA WILD!

SAVANNAH CITY MARKET | 27 BARNARD STREET | 912-790-WING (9464)

WILDWINGCAFE.COM

© John Alexander Photography

{ ATTENTION LAND LOVERS }

If you're more of a land-lover, and prefer to eat something besides seafood, we've got that too. There are decades worth of opinions about what makes good fried chicken. You'll have to taste for yourself to find your favorite. No matter where you find your food tour taking you, in Savannah, the locals love to eat. Whether you're looking for food to go with your live entertainment like they have at **Wild Wing Café** in City Market or you want to try international food with a Savannah twist like the Greek stylings at **Olympia Café**, there's something for everyone.

So as you sit down to feast in Savannah prepare to savor every last bite. Because in Savannah, you'll soon discover that food feeds the stomach just as much as it does the soul.

{ SEAFOOD IS AS MUCH A PART OF SAVANNAH AS COBBLESTONES, SQUARES & SPANISH MOSS }

"The service was fantastic..

You were incredibly well staffed. This was a complicated wedding and your staff was great. Every aspect ran so smoothly. Thanks so much for all your hard work and planning."

Sebrell Smith, Wedding Planner

We Travel!

Try our on-site catering or at the Savannah International Trade & Convention Center

We would love to discuss your event or wedding.

From black-tie dinners and business meetings to cultural attractions and entertainment events, **SAVOR...Savannah Catering** provides delicious cuisine that is freshly prepared with the perfect choice for the ambiance and needs of every client. Our highly trained culinary team will make any event a sophisticated affair with dishes that look beautiful and taste sublime.

Contact Gerry Helmly at **912.447.4069** or **ghelmly@savtcc.com**.
WWW.SAVORSMGSAVANNAH.COM

SAVOR...
Savannah
CATERING

What do you want to drink?

WHILE YOU'RE OUT ENJOYING ALL OF SAVANNAH, DON'T FORGET TO GRAB A COCKTAIL.
WE HAVE A STRONG HISTORY WITH LIBATIONS IN THIS CITY, AND A UNIQUE TAKE ON WHERE YOU CAN DRINK.

Imagine, you're hanging out with friends at one of our trendy bars. They decide they're moving on to check out the next spot. "Let me finish my cocktail," you protest. The bartender hands you a plastic cup and with a wink says, "Take it to go!" Baffled, you whisper, "But, isn't that illegal?" The bartender shakes her head and yells, "Welcome to Savannah!"

As one of only a few places in the United States with a law permitting public alcohol consumption in an open container, Savannah's reputation as a city that loves its liquor is well-earned, and there are no shortage of places to sample these libations.

If you want to learn how to craft, try a cocktail class at Congress Street 220 Up. You'll learn how to create classic cocktails from seasoned bartenders. The classes also provide a history of the Prohibition era in a speakeasy atmosphere.

Or, snap a picture of these recipes and create your own Savannah cocktail back home. *Cheers!*

{ CHATHAM ARTILLERY PUNCH }

THIS IS ONE COCTAIL THAT IS NOT FOR THE FAINT OF HEART — OR THE REALLY THRISTY —
SINCE IT IS BEST ENJOYED AFTER CHILLING FOR 2 DAYS.

Its namesake is part of history as it is known to possess a kick greater than the two brass cannons presented to the Chatham Artillery by George Washington. Feeling brave (or a little crazy?) Be sure to invite some friends over for this one!

INGREDIENTS

1 ½ gallons Catawba wine
½ gallon rum
1 quart gin
1 quart brandy
½ pint Benedictine
2 quarts Maraschino cherries

1 ½ quarts rye whiskey
1 ½ gallons strong tea
2 ½ pounds brown sugar
1 ½ quarts orange juice
1 ½ quarts lemon juice

Mix from 36 to 48 hours before serving. Add one case of champagne when ready to serve. (and more importantly, don't plan on going anywhere after bottoms up!). *Enjoy!*

{ OGLETHORPE'S MULE }

DRINK LIKE YOU FOUNDED SAVANNAH
WITH THIS TWIST ON THE CLASSIC MOSCOW MULE.

Oglethorpe's Mule is a perfect drink for Savannah's hot summer days. With the refreshing flavors of ginger, mint and lime mixed with locally distilled Ghost Coast Vodka 261, this cocktail will definitely cool you off.

INGREDIENTS

1 ½ oz Ghost Coast Vodka 261
¾ oz Lime Juice
¾ Ginger Syrup *(Or Ginger Beer)*
Club Soda
Mint Leaves

Shake first 3 ingredients, pour into copper mug or Collins glass, over ice, top with club soda. Garnish with Lime wheel and mint sprig. *Cheers!*

THE COCKTAIL ROOM

HAND-CRAFTED COCKTAILS
PREPARED BY SAVANNAH'S OWN

—SYDNEY LANCE

GHOST COAST DISTILLERY

GhostCoastDistillery.com

Gourmet Fun
AT THE SAVANNAH FOOD & WINE FESTIVAL

Savannah Food & Wine Festival

THE SOUTH'S BEST CULINARY HAPPENINGS - ONE EXCEPTIONAL WEEK IN SAVANNAH.

If ever there were a time to mark your calendar – this is it. Each November, for seven remarkable days, those lucky enough to secure tickets indulge in the Savannah Food & Wine Festival. Jam-packed doesn't begin to describe this foodie fairytale come true with more than 40 food-centric events taking place in just one week. From dinners by award-winning chefs in historic mansions to five-star fare in Savannah's historic backdrop, the culinary feats are nothing short of magnificent and every bit worth the annual wait.

HERE'S A GLIMPSE OF WHAT MAY AWAIT YOU AT THIS MUST-TASTE FESTIVAL:

{ CELEBRITY CHEF TOUR }
An incredibly rare and truly exquisite night.

For one evening, award-winning James Beard Chefs combine their extraordinary efforts, each preparing a course for this once-in-a-lifetime dinner. The Celebrity Chef Tour is the festival's most epic culinary event bringing diverse talents together for a magical, memorable and interactive dining experience. Much like dining at the James Beard House, guests of this event have the rare opportunity to interact with the participating chefs throughout the evening.

{ GRAND RESERVE TASTING }
If wine is your passion, this is your event!

The Grand Reserve Tasting is the showcase event for the very best wines. Guests are given a collectible piece of fine stemware to use throughout the night (and take home as a souvenir) as they sip a variety of vintages. To round out the evening, a silent auction is also held with such items up for bid as luxury travel, wine and more. So, raise a glass and reserve your tickets to this sell-out event sooner rather than later.

{ RIVER STREET STROLL }
An intimate evening of wine and spirits.

Savannah's famous River Street is best known for its historic cobblestone pavers, eighteenth-century buildings and sweeping river views. But on this night, the enjoyment of River Street is elevated to an entirely new level. During the River Street Stroll, attendees enjoy an intimate evening of wine and spirits, intermixed with the riverfront's culinary delights and shopping whimsy. It's quite possibly the best way to sip, savor and shop that you'll ever experience!

{ TASTE OF SAVANNAH }

Each year this is the main event of the Festival.

So big, in fact, that it has been expanded to Georgia Railroad Museum where all do their best to choose from hundreds of wine exhibitors, food booths, cooking demonstrations, celebrity cookbook signings and so much more! Some will come just for the food, others for the cooking demonstrations, while others want to experience it all! You too can take your pick from the many fabulous festivities! Pro-tip, buy your tickets earlier in the year for the best prices.

Though the chefs, the food and the wines may change, one thing is certain: every year the Savannah Food and Wine Festival continues to get better and better! Of course that also means it is gaining popularity so it is advised to make your plans early for this can't-miss event by visiting www.SavannahFoodandWineFestival.com. Updates are posted regularly as they become available and as history has shown us, the most popular events sell out fast – but trust us, you're going to want to take your time and savor every last bite. *Bon Appetit!*

FOR MORE INFORMATION ABOUT THE FESTIVAL OR TO PURCHASE TICKETS, VISIT **SAVANNAHFOODANDWINEFESTIVAL.COM**

BRINGING THE WORLD TO SAVANNAH

The Georgia Tech Savannah campus focuses on shaping the future vision for the coastal region. Through engaging the community and industries our curriculum provides education for its current and future workers. Creating custom courses for area corporate partners, bringing research, technology and resources from main campus and engaging in the innovation of the greater Savannah region, Georgia Tech Savannah is at the forefront in providing world class educational resources for the southeast.

Georgia Tech | Professional Education

savannah.gatech.edu

the *Tastes* of SAVANNAH

Nearly 20 years ago, the Taste of Savannah became the signature, must attend event to find out what restaurants were THE best places to taste.

Today, the event has evolved into the Who's-Who of Great Tastes. If your trip did not coincide with the festival this year, make plans for next year and enjoy a delectable taste at one of these great restaurants throughout the year.

45 bistro
123 E. Broughton Street
912.234.3111 • 45bistro.com

Five Oaks Taproom
201 W. Bay Street
912.236.4440 • fiveoakstaproom.com

Ben & Jerry's of Savannah
25 E Broughton St Suite 1B
912.421.2086 • benjerry.com

Belford's Savannah Seafood & Steaks
315 W. St. Julian Street
912.233.2626 • belfordssavannah.com

Pie Society
19 Jefferson Street
912.238.1144 • thebritishpiecompany.com

Congaree and Penn Farm & Mills
11830 Old Kings Road, Jacksonville, FL
904.527.1945 • congareeandpenn.com

Blowin' Smoke Southern Cantina
1611 Habersham Street
912.231.2385 • blowinsmokesavannah.com

Moss + Oak Savannah Eatery
2 West Bay Street
912.721.4510

The Chromatic Dragon
514 Martin Luther King, Jr. Boulevard
912.289.0350 • chromaticdragon.com

Pacci Italian Kitchen + Bar
601 E Bay Street
912.233.6002 • paccisavannah.com

Grand Champion BBQ
Four Atlanta Locations
770.587.4227 • gcbbq.com

Coastal Center for Developmental Services
1249 Eisenhower Drive
912.644.7500 • ccdssavannah.org

savannah: a southern journey | 83

Step Inside

THESE 3 SACRED SAVANNAH SPOTS

Savannah's first church service took place the very day General Oglethorpe docked his ship at the Yamacraw Bluff on February 12, 1733. It was attended by 120 new colonists and conducted by the general himself. Since then, Savannah's spiritual legacy has only gotten stronger and more storied.

These Savannah churches and synagogues are more than just places of worship. They're prime examples of gorgeous architecture with detailed artwork and rich histories.

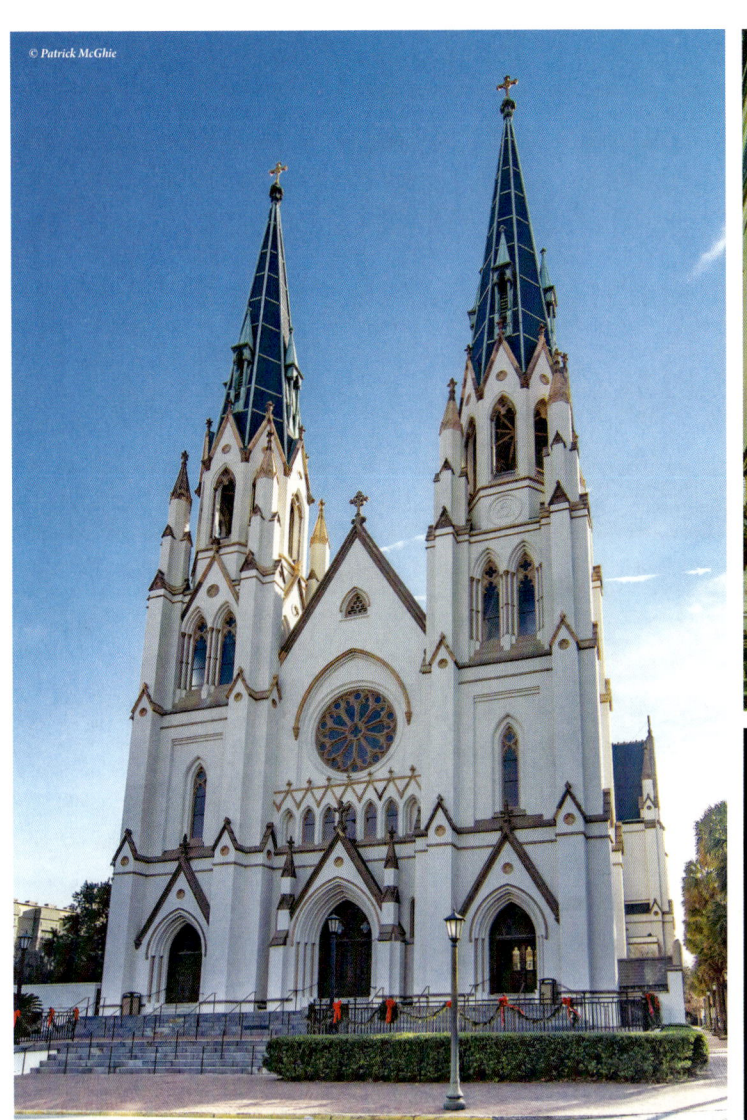

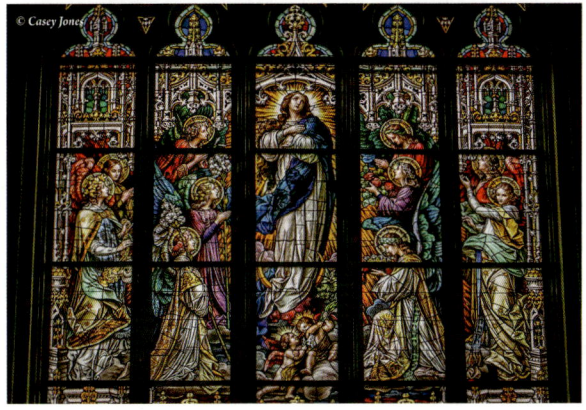

{ THE CATHEDRAL OF ST. JOHN THE BAPTIST }

The Cathedral of St. John the Baptist is known for being the "Sistine of the South" for good reason – it's filled with elaborate stained glass, tall marble-like columns and a presence that takes your breath away. The Cathedral's murals date back to 1912, and are actually oil on canvas paintings transferred to the church walls.

TOUR INFORMATION: The Cathedral is open for self-guided touring Monday through Saturday from 9 a.m. to 11:45 a.m. and 12:45 p.m. to 5 p.m. Tours are free, but a small donation for church upkeep and preservation is appreciated.

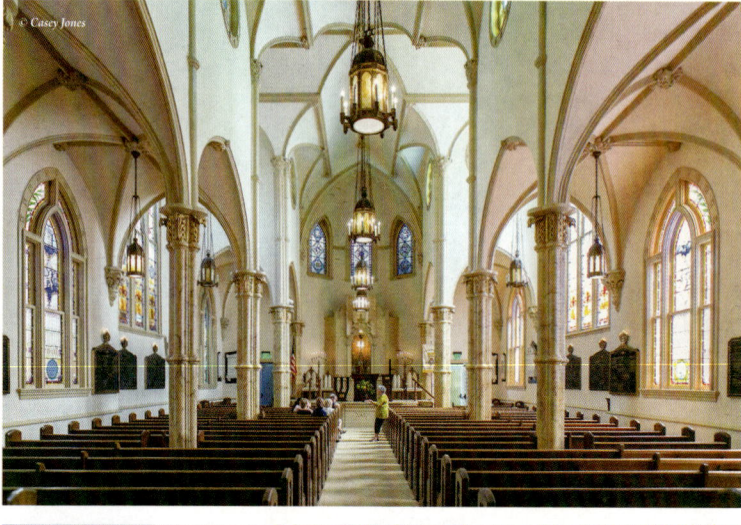

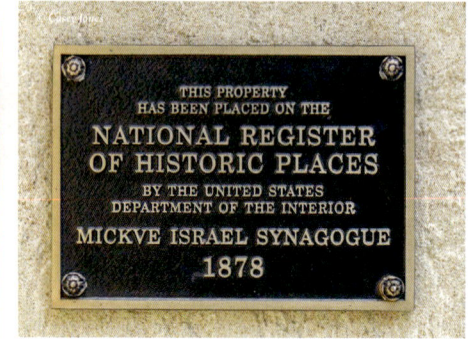

{ CONGREGATION MICKVE ISRAEL }

Founded in 1733, Congregation Mickve Israel is another important religious historical site. Mickve Israel is the third oldest Jewish congregation in America, setting up just a few months after the founding of the city of Savannah. Inside the synagogue is a small museum that includes an array of historic artifacts.

TOUR INFORMATION: The historic sanctuary and museum are open for tours Monday through Friday *(excluding Jewish and federal holidays)* from 10 a.m. to 1 p.m. and 2 p.m. to 4 p.m. Mickve Israel requests a donation to assist with upkeep and preservation.

86 | savannah: a southern journey

{ SECOND AFRICAN BAPTIST CHURCH }

Founded in 1802, the Second African Baptist Church is the historic African American Church where General Sherman made his well-known "Forty Acres and a Mule" proclamation from the church steps to the newly freed slaves. Civil rights activist Martin Luther King Jr. also visited this church.

TOUR INFORMATION: Currently, the church is open for group tours by reservation only.

THE LANDINGS
on Skidaway Island

SAVANNAH'S CHARM, EXCEPTIONAL AMENITIES AND LASTING FRIENDSHIPS...

Imagine the exhilarating lifestyle you've always dreamed of. A stunningly beautiful island community where neighbors make you feel at home *before you even arrive*. Golf, boating, sparkling waterways, parks, miles of trails, and a Club that specializes in 'special'. All mere minutes from the historic city of Savannah, Georgia. We've made it a reality at The Landings on Skidaway Island.

Visit and explore: 3 days/2 nights, $249/couple. TheLandings.com

TheLandings.com   (912) 598-0500   The Landings Company: One Landings Way North, Savannah, GA

6 PRIVATE GOLF COURSES—ONE MEMBERSHIP • 40 MILES OF WALKING & BIKING TRAILS • 2 DEEPWATER MARINAS
ACTIVE NEIGHBORS GROUPS • FITNESS & WELLNESS, 34 TENNIS COURTS & 5 POOLS • 4 CLUBHOUSES WITH FARM-TO-TABLE DINING

READY TO CALL SAVANNAH *Home?*

FOR THOSE WHO CAN'T GET ENOUGH OF SAVANNAH, HERE'S HOW YOU TURN YOUR VACATION INTO A REMARKABLE RELOCATION.

While the history and beauty of Savannah is likely what brought you here, it is the city's hospitality that will make you want to stay. Thankfully, the city and its nearby communities offer a magnificent choice of neighborhoods that will soon have you wanting to put down some permanent roots.

{ MIDTOWN }

Made up primarily of the Ardsley Park neighborhood, Midtown Savannah is iconic for its homes with Belgian block walls and Spanish-style roofed pillars that are as architecturally stunning today as when they were first constructed in 1909. Ardsley Park features many small parks that are neighborhood gathering places and beautiful focal points with playgrounds, picnic areas and a ball field. *(above)*

{ SOUTHSIDE, WEST CHATHAM & BEYOND }

For communities featuring newer construction, you'll find abundant options in Southside Savannah as well as areas just beyond the city limits including the up-and-coming community of Pooler. Outside Chatham County, Richmond Hill and Rincon are two great communities that are a stone's throw from Savannah.

{ ISLE OF HOPE }

Picture white picket fences and expansive coastal views and you will have envisioned Isle of Hope.
This quaint island features a variety of home styles that combine to form a truly authentic coastal community.

{ WILMINGTON, WHITEMARSH & TYBEE ISLAND }

Wilmington and Whitemarsh Islands feature a mix of estate-home communities as well as ranch-style homes and a variety of luxury apartments and condominiums. Nearby Tybee Island is best known for its beach cottages that will beckon you to slip off your shoes, sink into the sand and stay awhile.

{ THE LANDINGS }

Located on Skidaway Island, this private, gated community is less than a 20-minute drive from downtown but feels worlds away.
Home to six world-class golf courses, 34 tennis courts, two marinas (with access to the Intracoastal Waterway), four clubhouse restaurants,
40 miles of trails and a newly renovated 48,000-square-foot fitness center, the Landings offers superb Savannah living.

{ HISTORIC DOWNTOWN }

From historic homes remodeled to look like new, to new homes constructed to fit in with Savannah's historic appeal, living downtown puts you close to all of Savannah's culture and activity. To help hone in on your favorite locale, we recommend dividing your search into downtown's four well-known sections including the Historic Landmark District, Victorian District, Thomas Square/Starland and Baldwin Park. All of these neighborhoods will put you within walking and biking distance of some of Savannah's most iconic attractions. Who wouldn't want to stroll by the Forsyth Park Fountain every day?

GEORGIA'S BEST & BRIGHTEST

Choose Southern

GEORGIA SOUTHERN UNIVERSITY

96 | savannah: a southern journey

editor in chief
Molly Swagler

creative director
Abbi Carter Gravino

advertising
Ron Scalf

---

contributing writers
Jesse Blanco, Laura Clark, Heather Thompson Grant, Angela Hendrix, Allison Hersh, Jessica Leigh Lebos, Christine Lucas, Tim Rutherford, Claire Sandow, Larissa Allen, Taylor Castillejo, Visit Savannah Team and John Wetherbee

---

photographers
Ali Competiello, Alicia Briscoe, Alissa Nicholson, Angela Hopper, Annie Nemeth, Ashlee Wells, Attic Fire Photography, Bryan Stovall, Carrie Kellogg, Christy Jackson, Cindy Hornung, Donald Pearson, Helen Titshaw, Howard Hackney, Jason Manchester, Jim Raddatz, John Alexander, Judi Trahan, Kathy Salvatore, Kevin Banker, Linda Ferguson, Michael Grafton, Michael Toogood, Patrick McGhie, Rebecca Fenwick, Rodney Gary, Tim Welch, Timothy Lilley, Tracy Scarpati, Tracy Toogood and William Levitt

---

Published by the Tourism Leadership Council

www.tourismleadershipcouncil.com

P.O. Box 10010, Savannah, Georgia 31412

ISBN 978-0-692-97780-4

© Tourism Leadership Council 2018

TLC TOURISM
VISION · ADVOCACY · ACTION

All rights reserved. This book may not be reproduced on whole or in part, in any form, without permission from the publisher.

MIKIMOTO

Ω OMEGA

Historic Downtown